"There is no one better positioned to produce books on homicide and serial murder than Steve Daniels. Whether you are a novice of the homicide literature or an expert yourself, this book offers something for readers at all levels of homicide knowledge."

- Dirk C. Gibson
Associate Professor, University of New Mexico

"Steve Daniels draws on his expertise and years of experience to provide a stunning insight and in-depth look into serial killers and their victims. His unique perspective and assessment of the serial killer is brilliant."
- Sherry A. Hunter, MA, Probation and Parole Agent

"Steve's influence on the fields of homicide prevention and research, investigative training, and criminal profiling cannot be overlooked. As one of his former students, I can personally attest to the incredible accomplishment it is to learn from truly one of the most original and admired profilers of our time.
- Dr. Melissa Matuszak, PhD, D-ABMDI
Assistant Professor-Administration of Justice

I met Steve Daniels thirty years ago when he was presenting on Satanism. As I was working with parents of teens involved with many forms of youth subcultures, his knowledge was timely. Since that time, he has mentored me through many tough juvenile cases. His insights into their thinking helped me to develop strategies and a screening tool that saved many lives. Many parents owe him their gratitude.

- Kathy Sorenson
Parent Advocate and Juvenile Interventionist

Gazing Into the Abyss

Serial Killer William Zamastil, His Victims, and Other Killers

Steve Daniels

M&B Global Solutions, Inc.
Green Bay, Wisconsin (USA)

Gazing Into the Abyss
*Serial Killer William Zamastil,
His Victims, and Other Killers*

© 2018 Steve Daniels

First Edition
All Rights Reserved. The author grants no assignable permission to reproduce for resale or redistribution. This license is limited to the individual purchaser and does not extend to others. Permission to reproduce these materials for any other purpose must be obtained in writing from the publisher except for the use of brief quotations within book chapters.

Disclaimer
The views expressed in this work are solely those of the author. They do not necessarily reflect the views of the publisher, and the publisher hereby disclaims any responsibility for them. In the event you use any of the information in this book for yourself, which is your constitutional right, the author and the publisher assume no responsibility for your actions.

Front cover photo courtesy of the Wisconsin Department of Corrections.

ISBN-13: 978-1-942731-33-7
ISBN-10: 1-942731-33-7

Published by M&B Global Solutions Inc.
Green Bay, Wisconsin (USA)

Dedication

To my entire family

Chris and Kristin
Joshua and Isaac
Joe and Abbey
Zooey and Pearl

And mostly to my wife, Nancy

Contents

Introduction 1
Chapter 1 - *Mary: His Last Victim* 5
Chapter 2 - *What is a Serial Killer?* 13
Chapter 3 - *The Serial Killer in Wisconsin* 33
Chapter 4 - *The Player in the Hunt* 47
Chapter 5 - *Who the Hell is William Zamastil?* 55
Chapter 6 - *Christine: Was She the First Victim?* . 65
Chapter 7 - *Zamastil's Other Known and Suspected Victims* 75
Chapter 8 - *Is There Such a Thing as a Serial Killer Wannabe?* 91
Chapter 9 - *Do We Need a New Category of Multiple Murder?* 107
Acknowledgements 137
About the Author 139

> *"Murder is an inherently evil act, no matter what circumstances, no matter how convincing the rationalizations."*
>
> **- Author Bentley Little**

> *"I long for the taste of blood."*
>
> **- William Zamastil, on the cell block, according to a corrections officer**

Introduction

The collective serial killer is a rapacious monster with an unquenchable appetite for human misery and destruction. You will see this time and again in this book.

The primary antagonist is a little-known, Wisconsin-born serial killer named William Zamastil, but he will not be the total focus of this writing. Instead, this book features an overview of the serial killer phenomenon and I will refer to many killers in the following pages. Veteran crime readers, as well as those new to the genre, will be introduced to updated research along with some new theories. Zamastil, himself, will be discussed in relatively general terms as part of a greater menace that has been with us since earlier times.

It is common practice for the media and others to refer to serial killers by their complete names such as John Wayne Gacy, Henry Lee Lucas, David Parker Ray, and Westley Alan Dodd. This simply sets them apart, almost as if to honor them. Zamastil's middle name will not be used in this book, nor will the middle names of any other killers. They simply do not deserve the adulation.

As Zamastil would not cooperate with this project, this is an unauthorized story. It is another reason he is not doted upon. This does not prevent the presentation of an accurate sketch of this killer, along with others of his ilk.

The known victims of Zamastil will be featured, and the crimes discussed, debated, and dissected. In one famous unsolved case, there remains a deep debate regarding Zamastil's guilt. This determination will be left for you to discuss, opine, and decide.

Gazing into the Abyss: Serial Killer William Zamastil, His Victims and Other Killers is not intended to be a gore fest. I will attempt to address the murders perpetrated by Zamastil with dignity whenever possible. Obviously, some crime particulars might be somewhat lurid, but will be necessary to offer the reader a glimpse into Zamastil's psyche as well as that of other killers. In order to know this killer, you need to know what he is capable of, but gruesomeness will be held in check. As the great FBI profiler, John Douglas offered, "In order to know the artist, you must study his work."

The last chapter in this book emanates from a discussion among crime students. It began as an idea for further review, then morphed into an article which was temporarily shelved. Now, due to the subject matter of the other chapters, it was deemed relevant to the overall discussion of serial murder. Hopefully it adds to the give and take among readers.

Some chapters will include discussion questions at the end so that groups might engage in dialogue about the subject matter. Also, I encourage you to research many of the other killers mentioned in the book.

Steve Daniels

"The monstrous act by definition demands a monster."

- Author Rick Yancey

Chapter 1

Mary: His Last Victim

On August 1, 1978, a young man promised to take his part-time girlfriend and her children school shopping. He phoned the girl late that afternoon, informing her his car had broken down and he would need a ride to fulfill his shopping promise. Agreeing to pick him up, she drove to a gas station and found him drinking beer and clutching a suitcase. She drove him to her house, where he continued his heavy consumption of alcohol, falling asleep on the couch. The young woman was getting antsy to shop and awakened him.

Ornery and still drunk, the man agreed to take her to Copps Department Store. On the way, he opened the suitcase and removed two handguns, a .38 caliber and a .45 caliber. He ordered her to drive on back roads, then proceeded to fire his guns out of the passenger-side window. Shell casings flew into the back seat, where the woman's two children were seated. The woman hollered at the shooter, imploring him to cease his firing.

He complied just as they arrived at the department store at around 5:00 p.m. The woman and her children separated from the man to shop, and when finished they waited for him to return to the designated spot. They left when he failed to return.

***

Mary Johnson. A plain name. A simple name. A name that is legion. But unlike many other Mary Johnsons, it was also the name of a pretty young woman murdered in Sauk County, Wisconsin, in 1975.

Mary, a vivacious twenty-four-year-old, had most of her life ahead of her. She was working, enjoying life, and was deep in the happy throes of planning a wedding to her boyfriend of approximately four years. The ceremony was scheduled for August 5, 1978, in Stevens Point, Wisconsin. Nearly 150 people were invited. But it was not to happen. Instead, a different ceremony was to occur.

This sparkling woman was described by friends as an "attractive, auburn-haired sprite," as she stood only five feet, one inch. She worked at Copps Department Stores' corporate office in Stevens Point and had transferred to a Madison, Wisconsin, store to be closer to her fiancé. The store manager described her as a good employee, friendly, outgoing, and polite.

Crimes Against Mary

On August 1, 1978, at approximately 5:15 p.m., Mary had finished her shift and was heading out for the evening. She was walking to her car, a blue 1977 Mustang. Upon reaching the vehicle, a man approached her and produced a handgun. He made Mary move to the passenger seat of her automobile. She was being abducted.

The predator, in a written and then taped statement, offered, "I drove around for about forty-five minutes talking to the girl." He then drove to the little town of Sauk City in the southern part of the state. They arrived at his destination, August W. Derleth Park, a beautiful, pristine wooded area. The abductor took a .45 automatic from his suitcase in the backseat and forced Mary to walk with him down a path to the river. There the pair, predator and prey, talked for another thirty to forty minutes.

It was during this conversation that Mary informed her captor that she was to be married the following Saturday. That was when the man told her to get undressed. According to him, Mary pleaded what could be the universal thought of those about to be hurt, stating, "I don't care what you do, just don't hurt me."

The man told Mary to lie down and she complied. He unzipped his pants, took them off and forced sex on his captive. It was at this time that Mary uttered the second universal thought of those about to not be released: "If you let me go, I won't tell anyone."

The .45 gun was in plain sight during the sexual assault. When he was finished, the rapist stood up and told Mary to roll over onto her stomach. Then, while straddling her, he jacked a round into the gun's chamber. Hearing this sound, Mary turned to look at him, then put her head back down, now certain of what her fate was to be. The killer shot Mary one time in the back of the neck. He stood up, gazed at his conquest, admired his work, and then headed to the car.

Mary had been raped and murdered. Hers was a broken body left like debris in the flora of the park.

While walking back to the car, the murderer noticed his wallet was not in his back pocket. He began to return to the crime scene, then thought better of it and walked to the car. He drove off in his victim's car with two guns inside, and later stopped at a fast food restaurant to discard his shirt.

The killer then phoned an off-duty Dane County Sheriff's Deputy, David Storley, telling him, "I'm in big trouble ... I shot a girl." Storley, who knew the killer from a previous jail stint, suggested they meet at a Madison shopping center. Another officer was called as backup. When Storley met the confessing offender, he learned the man had left an injured woman in Derleth Park. Mary's body was found immediately and the suspect placed into custody.

Dane County authorities had already been looking for a perpetrator in regard to another shooting; this time involving the firing of two guns out the window of a car in which he had forced a woman to drive him around while he drank. There was much property damage, but no human injury. These were the same guns shown to Mary in the process of her abduction. Following that initial incident, the shooter ordered the driver to drop him off in the parking lot of the Copps store where Mary worked, and the horrendous events of the night ensued.

Finding Her Body and the Investigation

Deputy Storley contacted the Sauk County authorities immediately and Mary's body was quickly located by a patrol deputy. After securing the brutal scene, three officers conducted a line search of the area. The first deputy on-site maintained a chain of evidence, remaining near the body for a couple of hours. Professionals from the Wisconsin State Crime Laboratory arrived on scene at 4:20 a.m., August 2, 1978, and began documenting and photographing the body as well as the surrounding area.

Mary was found as the killer had left her: nude, lying on her stomach, with a bullet hole in her neck and head tucked in the crook of her arm. She was located about fifty yards off a footpath, splayed out as in a deep sleep. Some clothing was by her side and some was bundled at her feet between her legs. A pair of panties lay under her body. There, in plain sight between her feet, lay the wallet of the killer containing the Arizona driver's license for the suspect.

Removal of the Body

After the lab personnel had completed their preliminary documentation of the scene, arrangements were made with a local funeral home to transport Mary's body to University Hospital in Madison for an autopsy to be performed by well-known forensic pathologist Dr. Robert W. Huntington III. Huntington was a brusque, bearded (no moustache), and disheveled man who looked like he would be more at ease in a lumberjack camp than in a lab setting.

The first deputy on the murder scene was charged with accompanying the body from the time it was placed in the ominous, black-zippered bag until it was turned over to the pathologist.

The Autopsy

Huntington's gross anatomical diagnosis outlined the following: a gunshot wound to the neck, severing of the spinal cord; penetration of the left carotid artery; exit wound left exterior of the neck. There were also posterior and superior lacerations to the vaginal area. Hemorrhaging of the larynx was also present.

The manner of death was listed as a homicide. The cause: a single gunshot wound to the neck striking the windpipe and spinal cord. Other notes indicated possible strangulation and trauma to the genitals.

The Investigation

After obtaining a formal confession, there was little left to investigate. Prosecutors needed to put their case in order for trial. Along with the killer's written and taped confession, items found at the crime scene were entered into evidence: various IDs with the suspect's name, pay stubs, and driver's license. Also located were a .45 shell casing from a gun stolen from his brother, Mary's employee badge, her clothing, and a work smock.

Items gathered from a search of Mary's car included a revolver, a .45 automatic with one shell in the chamber, and four shells in a clip. Three suitcases holding an array of the killer's clothing were found in the back seat.

Court

Mary's killer was found guilty of premeditated murder, first degree sexual assault, and kidnapping. He received the following sentence structure: premeditated murder, life in prison; first degree sexual assault, twenty years; and kidnapping, twenty years, for a total sentence of life plus forty years.

Sadly, Mary was laid to rest on the same day she was to be married. She was murdered by the serial killer William Zamastil, the scourge of many and the main predator in this book.

"They are spores and bedlamites."

- From the BBC crime drama "Luther"

Chapter 2

What is a Serial Killer?

Although serial murder likely has been with us since the dawn of humankind, the definition of this criminal phenomenon is relatively new. All multiple-victim homicides were labeled mass murder in the early years of study, but then this unique variety of murder broke into people's consciousness and a new term was needed to differentiate the various types of murder. Over the years, the meaning of serial murder has changed, mutated, and begged for a solid, workable definition.

Defining Serial Murder

It appears that the Federal Bureau of Investigation (FBI) was the first American law enforcement entity to define the serial killer. In the 1988 groundbreaking book, Sexual Homicide, the authors defined serial murder as "three or more victims, murdered by the same perpetrator, with a cooling off period between killings, and the murders are most often driven by a sexual fantasy." The cooling off period is the time between the offenses where the killer is sexually sated. It could be days, weeks, or even years as in such cases as the still-uncaught Zodiac killer of Northern California, or the Bind, Torture, Kill (BTK perpetrator), the nefarious specter from Wichita, Kansas. These types of homicides were originally labeled lust murders. The serial murder term offered criminologists a new idea to study: a killer who is often cunning, planning and stalking their potential victims.

Steve Giannangelo, in his book *Real Life Monsters*, suggests that the definition of serial murder is often based on "specific parameters, such as victimology, geographic location, and victim-killer relationship." It seems that students of this type of crime have settled on a variation of the FBI's definition, counting two murders instead of three. In fact, at a recent FBI-sponsored conference to define a common, usable definition for serial killers, the proposed definition requires "the presence of at least one offender, two or more victims, two or more murder incidents, and a time period between murders." This proposal is much more inclusive than previous definitions.

Types of Serial Murder

Many researchers, criminologists, and criminal justice professionals differ in their approaches to type serial murder. Miki Pistorius, the first person in South Africa to write a dissertation on serial murder and the first profiler for the South African National Police, based her types of killers on Freud's id, ego, and super-ego phases. She offers that a killer fixates on a particular stage of Freudian psychosexual development, and then acts it out in a murder. Pistorious, according to some documentation, feels she has "cryptesthesia," an extra sense or type of clairvoyance, when dealing with serial killers.

Richard Walter, the internationally renowned "modern Sherlock Holmes," formerly of the Vidocq Society (a members-only crime-solving club), along with Robert Keppel, lead investigator in the Ted Bundy case, delineate types of serial killers by using the four categories of rapists/murderers. These categories most often pertain to males as the perpetrators and women as the victims.

1) Power Reassurance – The person lacks confidence in his ability to interact sexually with women. He does not intentionally degrade or traumatize the victim, and might even apologize.

2) Power Assertive – Feels he has the right to rape. A macho-man type, and might use repeated, violent attacks.

3) Anger Retaliatory – Gets even with women for perceived wrongs. Rape is an unplanned, blitz attack using weapons of convenience; i.e., arms, legs. Feels relief when done.

4) Anger Excitation – Primary motivation is to inflict pain/suffering. Brutal force can be used and the victim usually dies. Victim is bound and taken to a pre-selected site where weapons, torture tools, and recording devices are often used.

The FBI developed its typology after what was at the time a comprehensive study of serial killers based on interviews of thirty-six convicted killers. They divided killers into two groups: disorganized non-social, and organized asocial. (Since the original research project in the late 1980s, many more killers have been interviewed and added to the study pool.)

Disorganized Non-Social

This offender is often typically a social isolate, a misfit residing alone in a hovel-type abode or with parents in a basement-like room. There is harsh discipline in the home and the father has an unstable work history. The killer is of low intelligence, has a menial job, and few friends, usually younger than he is. This offender did not do well in high school, if even completing it. He most likely lives near the crime scene and quite possibly does not own car.

His crime is very impulsive, the crime scene is a mess, and the weapon is one of opportunity. The body is left at the scene, and there is often evidence of necrophilia and post-mortem experimentation. The victim is one of convenience or opportunity. Richard Chase, the "Vampire of Sacramento," is an example of this type of killer. This emaciated young man was extremely mentally ill and felt aliens had tainted his blood. In his twisted mind, he felt he needed fresh blood, which drove him to murder six persons and engage in necrophilia, cannibalism, mutilation, and blood-drinking.

Organized Asocial

This killer is the polar opposite of the disorganized offender. He is well-versed, often handsome, and charming. He might be married and is popular within his crowd. He can stalk victims as he has a car in good working order. This man follows the crime in the media and could possibly try to ingratiate himself into the investigation by drinking in bars that cater to off-duty police, even volunteering to help search or pass out flyers.

His offense is pre-planned, with a targeted, specific victim. In fact, one offender was so murderously sophisticated that he would enter the homes of pre-selected victims when they were away. He would scour the house to get the lay of the land, then hide ropes, shoelaces, or zip ties for later use when returning to the chosen home. Restraints are often used, as well as a personal "murder kit." This often consists of restraints, a mask, weapon, prophylactics, and other items to be employed in the commission of a sexual murder.

The offender's vehicle could be modified so that once inside, the victim could not escape. The body could be transported or hidden. This offender can be extremely difficult to apprehend and his killing could go on for years.

Ted Bundy could be the prototype for this type of killer, as well as Ed Kemper, the killer of female hitchhikers.

Gary Hinton was an organized, brazen, and very sophisticated offender who lured or located hikers in southern forests, held them captive, and then murdered them. While the killings were occurring, Hinton approached a filmmaker with an idea for a movie. The star could lure women into the forest, hold them captive, then hunt them down and murder them. He even located a spot for the shooting of the movie not far from one of his killings. The movie was *Deadly Run*, released in 1995.

Another convicted serial killer, Rodney Alcala, was so glib, suave, and cultured that he was actually a contestant on television game shows, including *The Dating Game*.

Todd Kohlhepp, a serial shooter full of bravado, was convicted of murdering seven people in South Carolina between 2003 and 2016. Upon his arrest, he was in possession of huge amounts of high-tech weaponry as well as copious amounts of ammunition. This killer described the murders with great relish. He demeaned investigators by boasting about his police-like skills. He told the detectives that in his quadruple homicide, he "cleared the room," (killed the victims) with SWAT-like precision unlike anything they had seen. He also bragged about his speed in reloading his weapon in the midst of the carnage, while not allowing a single victim to escape. He told investigators, "You would have been impressed."

Although it is rare, a single killer might exhibit qualities of both an organized and disorganized killer at the crime scene, as well as during commission of a murder. This phenomenon is labeled as mixed. The person seems to mix and match the better of one category with the worst of the other. A mixed scene might also indicate more than one offender.

Holmes Typology

Ronald Holmes, a criminologist and former coroner, categorizes serial murder in four specific types and three subsets, often including the motives.

1) Visionary – This killer is very likely psychotic and not totally in touch with reality. He kills in response to voices or visions that lead him to a certain type or group of persons to be eliminated. Many express that the voice is that of God ordering them to rid the earth of evil. This could be in the form of prostitutes, runaways, drug addicts; basically society's "throw-aways." In some instances, it could be family members. Criminologist Steve Egger called them "the less than dead," because they were considered less than living and were rarely missed by society. Harvey Carnigan, known as "Hammering Harvey," said he killed people by order of God. Joseph Kallinger, known as "The Shoemaker," said that after talking with God as well as a disembodied head, he murdered his son and three other individuals.

2) Mission-Oriented – This offender has a specific goal of getting rid of a select group of people, but sees no visions and hears no voices. He considers himself on a "mission," often quasi-military, to eliminate these peoples. Racial minorities, people of the Jewish faith, or homosexuals are examples. To him, these people are unworthy of life. Joseph Franklin, a long distance serial killer, murdered blacks, Jews, and interracial couples using a high-powered rifle. His goal was to make America white and racially pure. He also attempted to murder Larry Flynt, the publisher of *Penthouse Magazine*, for showing interracial couples engaged in sex in his magazine. Vernon Jordan, head of the Urban League was also a victim.

3) Hedonistic – His ultimate goal is personal pleasure or thrill-seeking. Each kill stokes his ego, rewarding him for a job well done. A total quest for pleasure drives him to continue killing. William Zamastil falls into this category, as does Richard Ramirez, the Night Stalker. Although Ramirez stole items from his victims, his main purpose for killing was the rush.

Here are three subsets to the Hedonistic category, according to Holmes:

1) Thrill-seeking – The pleasure emanates from the killing event. In describing the event, the offender is visibly excited and could very well be in a heightened state of sexual arousal. Brandon Wilson, mentioned in a later chapter, fits this subset.

2) Lust – This is killing for sexual gratification.

3) Comfort Lifestyle – This is murder to enhance the "good life." The murder is a tool toward attaining a more comfortable life, such as collecting insurance on murdered children or spouses. One bartending serial killer, Joe Ball, fed a number of his staff to his pet alligators to collect the staff members' paychecks or to refrain from paying them altogether.

4) Power/Control-Oriented – He loves playing God, holding the absolute power over life and death in his hands. The thrill is the power. This individual might bring a victim to near death and then revive them. The victim becomes a pawn relying on the largesse of the killer for his or her life. Often, these types of killers are sadistic in nature and collectors of humans. Leonard Lake and Charles Ng, who built and maintained a torture bunker in Northern California to hold captured sex slaves, fit this category, as does Robert Berdella Jr., the "Kansas City Butcher," who kept young men imprisoned in his house, naked and in dog collars.

Other Possible Theories

Captain Thomas Cronin (Ret.) offered other categories to explain serial killing to his students during detective in-services. His first typology list consisted of four combinations of factors that assist in labeling:

Specific Victims/Specific Methods – The aforementioned Ted Bundy was this type. Victims often looked similar and were killed and disposed of in the same way.

Two extremely interesting cases that fit this category, but fall outside the realm of "usual" serial killings, are those of De Mau Mau in the Chicago area, and the Death Angels in San Francisco, known as the Zebra murders, both occurring in the 1970s. Members of De Mau Mau were dishonorably discharged African American Vietnam veterans who killed nine victims, all white, including two mass slayings of families. All of the killings took place in the Chicago area and all victims were shot.

The Zebra killings (labeled as such as this was the police radio code) were another series of murders in San Francisco perpetrated by black men against white victims. These murders were also racially motivated. Although some authorities feel there could be as many as seventy victims, the four men convicted had a victim count totaling fifteen dead and ten wounded. All but two of the victims were shot.

Variety of Victims/Specific Methods – David Bullock killed six individuals, shooting them all in New York City. One was his roommate; others were an actor, investment banker, and a woman who laughed at him, among others. In court, he told the judge that murder made him happy.

Specific Victims/Variety of Methods – Although all of his victims were prostitutes, Richard Cottingham used different methods on many of them, including stabbing, strangling, and burning. He often tortured his victims and took body parts as trophies. His murders occurred in New Jersey.

Variety of Victims/Variety of Methods – Self-styled Satanist and cocaine addict Richard Ramirez killed a variety of people: elderly, young, Asian, white. It really didn't matter to him. He shot, stabbed, and strangled his way to infamy in the Los Angeles area.

The next method of listing serial killers by Capt. Cronin was by locale, a type of geographical profiling. He describes three subsets.

Place-Specific Killers – These individuals attempt to lure their prey to a specific location, such as their home, in order to do the killing. John Gacy was this type, killing in his home and burying victims in his narrow, dirt-filled crawl space. Gacy would lure young gay men to his home, ply them with alcohol and pornography, and then seduce them into a "magic" handcuff trick. Their fate was sealed.

Local Serial Killers – These perpetrators remain in a specific state, city or area. Albert DeSalvo, the "Boston Strangler," killed in and around the Boston area. David "Son of Sam" Berkowitz murdered couples on lovers' lanes in New York City.

Traveling Serial Killers – These men roam the United States in search of victims, often driving hundreds of miles from one killing spot to another. Henry Lucas might be the epitome of this type, often driving thousands of miles to murder. William Zamastil is also a member of this group, with known victims in Wisconsin, Arizona, and California. There can be large numbers of victims for this type, especially if law enforcement does not collaborate or notice a pattern.

Serial killer expert Mike Newton offers similar descriptors as Cronin, but with a somewhat different bent. He suggests the following categories:

Territorial Serial Killers – These murderers lay claim to a defined area of a county or city, or a smaller area within a locale such as a park or a neighborhood. They rarely venture from these killing fields. For example, David Berkowitz haunted lovers' lanes only within New York City.

Stationary Serial Killers – Newton paints a picture of a "spider in wait" for a select victim, such as a nursing home resident or a hospital patient.

Nomadic Serial Killers – These are vagabonds, a breed with no boundaries or ties to a singular place, moving from location to location in search of the "perfect" kill. Robert Silveria Jr. was a member of the Freight Train Riders of America, a hobo gang traversing the United States by riding the rails. Silveria, also known as "The Boxcar Killer," murdered as many as fourteen other hobos.

Using various subject categories, William Zamastil would be a disorganized, hedonistic, traveling serial killer using a mixture of weapons and hunting a variety of victims. In essence, his were a hodge-podge of killing thoughts, styles, and methods. Some true crime bloggers have suggested there is a stark similarity between Zamastil's killings and those of the Zodiac, the still-uncaptured California serial killer.

Although the Zodiac appeared more sophisticated, careful and brazen, there are some glaring similarities. Both used a variety of weapons. Both targeted a mixture of victims. Both were active in California and both victimized hitchhikers, but there the similarities seem to end.

Although many serial killers emanate from similar backgrounds, there is no such thing as serial killer typology template; no one-size-fits-all definition. Adding to the confusion is a current move by scholars to change the terminology away from serial murder. According to the Atypical Homicide web page, a number of individuals who have researched, written about, and assisted police agencies with cases offer different terminology. Matt DeLisi suggests "multiple homicide offender," Enzo Yaksic and Mike Aarmodt propose "multiple event murderer," and Sasha Reid coined the term "compulsive criminal homicide."

Case Briefs

Many persons with a casual or serious interest in the phenomenon known as the serial killer often mistakenly believe this is a new creature in the criminal lexicon. Certainly, the 1960s brought the serial killer up close and personal. The likes of Richard Speck in Chicago and Charles Manson in California escorted us into the following decades, which then brought us Ted Bundy, Henry Lucas, John Gacy, Richard Ramirez, and hundreds of others like them. Researchers label the 1980s as the height of the serial killer phenomenon, but new killers seem to be appearing in the news on a consistent basis.

The Act of Serial Murder

The late criminologist Joel Norris, among others, states that serial murder is an addiction or a disease, and as such has seven phases of development. His theory is not widely accepted by other serial killer researchers in total, but in some shape or form, the phases, albeit under different terminology, seem to appear in many serial killings. The phases according to Dr. Norris:

The Aura Phase – This is when the killer seems to lose a grip on reality and has a heightened sense of surroundings. The perverse, invasive, and sexually aberrant fantasy is intense.

The Trolling Phase – Simply put, this is hunting for a victim. It could be a random spot or a favored locale. It could be something as simple as driving up and down a road.

The Wooing Phase – If the attack is not a blitz-type, then the offender attempts to get in the graces of the victim by some type of ruse. He may be asking for directions or feigning an injury.

The Capture – Whether enticing a victim into a van, breaking into a house, or some other method, the victim is ensnared.

The Murder – The actual act of taking a life.

The Totem Phase – Attempting to "hang on" to the pleasure experienced during the killing. This could entail revisiting the crime scene or taking souvenirs from the victim. It could be keeping a scrapbook of the killing covered in the media or keeping a body part. It also could include ingratiating himself into the police investigation, such as passing out fliers or assisting in the search for the "missing" victim.

The Depression Phase – The murder is over. The aforementioned totems no longer fill the void. The oncoming aura stage has not yet appeared, so the malaise has crept back in. A letter might be sent to the police or a call to the victim's family might ensue. Remorse, if any, might rise to the surface in this phase.

A Brief History of Serial Murder

Forensic historians have learned that the presence of serial killers reaches back into the early stages of our history as a nation, spanning centuries like a plague that survives all attempts to quell it. The following is offered as a short list of lesser-known episodic killers in America's history.

Micajah ("Big") and Wiley ("Little") Harpes – These were cousins who masqueraded as brothers. Bedecked in fur caps, buckskins, and carrying muskets, hatchets and hunting knives, they resembled yetis wearing the pelts of their prey. During the late 1700s, this duo of death killed victims from Illinois to Kentucky, Mississippi, and Tennessee. Many students of crime consider this pair to be this country's first serial killers.

These "brothers" knew little loyalty, first fighting for the British, then absconding and joining a band of Native Americans. No matter what their "allegiance" of the moment, it seemed the lust for criminality and violence overwhelmed them, opening the doors to rape, arson, and looting. It was the raw desire to kill that brought "Big" and "Little" their exhilarating thrills. Victims were myriad, from babies to children, parents, and elderly, and single killings to entire families.

History has not been kind to the Harpes cousins, nor their escapades. This pair wreaked havoc on a new nation reeling from the Revolutionary War that broke the British yoke of imperialism. The war left many casualties, but so did the cousins. Their victims served no purpose other than to fulfill their quest for evil.

John, Ma, John Jr., and Kate Bender – The Benders rained havoc on the dusty roads of Labette County, Kansas, from 1872-73. This was a rural family spawned from the recesses of Hell. Luring lone travelers to their evil "inn," the Benders would bait, board, and butcher those hapless travelers.

Using beguiling twenty-two-year-old daughter Kate as a lure, the family would invite lone travelers, mostly men, to spend the night in their one-room inn, promising comfort, food, and a room. Kate would engage the lonely men, who were sitting above a trap door, while John Jr. or Pa would stand behind a curtain dividing the lone room. At the most opportune moment, they would either bludgeon the victim or cut his throat. A rough estimate of victims totals more than eleven. Many were identified; however, a few remain nameless. Body parts were found but never linked to any named dead.

Espinoza Brothers – The brothers came riding through Southwestern history in the spring of 1863 like cowboy demons on a human corpse round-up. Felipe and Jose Espinoza led a gang consisting of their cousins, dubbing themselves the "Bloody Espinozas." After witnessing the killing of six of their family members at the hands of the United States Military, the band of cut-throats relocated to the Colorado territory with vengeance in their hearts and blood-lust in their souls.

The first victim was found in May 1863. His heart was cut out and the body was mutilated. While a specific count of victims eludes history, twenty-five is a number believed to be accurate. Legend has it that Felipe had a vision of the Blessed Virgin telling him to kill 100 Anglos for every one of their family members killed, in what they considered the American Genocide of Manifest Destiny.

Jesse Pomeroy – In 1871-72, there were reports of young male victims being enticed and lured to extremely remote areas of Massachusetts by an older, milky-eyed boy named Jesse. These young victims were mercilessly beaten with fists, belts, and on occasion, a knife. Ruth Pomeroy, Jesse's mother, moved to Boston in 1872 and the attacks continued in this new location. Finally arrested, Jesse, a slow-witted, semi-blind youth, was convicted and sent to a juvenile facility until he turned eighteen.

Upon his release, Jesse began his reign of terror anew. This time not only did he assault other youth, he murdered them. In March 1874, Jesse abducted Katie Curran, a twelve-year-old girl, and murdered her, hiding her body in an ash heap in the basement of his mother's dress shop. Then, in April of the same year, the mutilated body of four-year-old Horace Millen was found in a marsh in South Boston. Not only was the facial area targeted, but more importantly, the eyes. Jesse was immediately suspected and led the police to the body.

J. Frank Hickey – This offender, known as "The Postcard Killer" due to the postcards he mailed to police and the media referencing the murders, killed three individuals and attacked twelve more from 1883-1912. His first kill was a co-worker at a drugstore using poison. He later obtained a job at a YMCA, which gave him access to a victim pool of choice, young boys. He murdered Michael Kruk in New York's Central Park, followed by the attempted murder of a young boy. On one occasion, Hickey was caught strangling a boy in plain view. Two months later, Hickey killed Joey Joseph and dumped his body down a latrine.

Herman Mudgett (aka H.H. Holmes) – Beginning in 1893, during the hub-bub of the World's Columbian Exposition in Chicago, Holmes took to building what became known as a "murder castle" within walking distance of the exposition. The castle was a maze of blind alleys, dead ends, trap doors, killing rooms, and an oven. All had the express purpose of luring gullible visitors to a world of unimaginable terror, panic, hysteria, and eventually death in myriad ways. Each was designed to satisfy Holmes's quest for personal ecstasy and added income. Some sources give his tally of victims as more than 200. Some pseudo-criminologists pose that Holmes was the elusive Jack the Ripper, come to America to ply his ghastly trade. But by most professional accounts, this is simply erroneous and offers no credence.

Martha Beck and Raymond Hernandez – Known as the "Lonely Hearts Killers," this duo of death brought the act of scouring love-wanted ads in newspapers by romance-starved women to a new low. Hernandez, a ne'er-do-well and slacker who fancied himself a gigolo, responded to an ad posted by Beck, and off to murder-land they traveled. Beck was an obese, slouch of a woman, who was smitten by her new Romeo, Hernandez. She gave up her kids, and together they laid waste to at least twenty unsuspecting women.

Students of serial murder should take the time to research some of the lesser-known, multiple incident murderers. Among them are: Joseph Kondro, Paul Runge, Robert Spangler, Felix Vail, Charlie Brandt, Gary Hilton, Robert Durst, and Joseph Nasco. These not-so infamous hunters of humans can offer added glimpses into the netherworld of killings.

Steve Daniels
Question

With all the information collected, studied, and researched, are we no closer to determining what a serial killer actually is? Is it a monster, Frankenstein-like creature, culled together with the worst bits and pieces of nurture vs. nature? Or are they bad seeds, damaged from the moment they experienced conception, aberrations of internal wiring? Or as one lay man offered, "Do they just pop out broken?"

"Something Wicked This Way Comes"

- Author Ray Bradbury

Chapter 3

The Serial Killer in Wisconsin

Most true crime aficionados would volunteer places such as California, Washington, Oregon, Texas, or Florida as the most common locations where serial killers commit their heinous acts. And rightly so, as this collection of states seems to produce an inordinate number of this type of offender.

Wisconsin, the state that produced William Zamastil, is not as prolific as other locales in the pantheon of serial killers, yet there is a list of infamous killers from the Badger State who have left an atlas of death across the landscape. There have been at least eleven serial killers in Wisconsin's history, likely many more. Regardless of the exact figure, Wisconsin has produced some of America's most notorious serial killers.

What follows is a smattering of these headline-grabbing Wisconsin cases and the killers who perpetrated them.

Ed Gein

Following in the footsteps of William Hare and William Burke, the noted nineteenth-century Scottish grave robbers (and murderers), Gein dug up the deceased not to sell, as Burke and Hare did, but to wallow in a perverted sexuality.

Gein was a socially stilted ghoul. He was a corpse thief, personified as one-third of the Buffalo Bill character in the movie *The Silence of the Lambs*. (The other two parts of that persona were Ted Bundy, who used the ruse of a broken arm to lure Good Samaritan victims into his sphere of death, and the other was Gary Heidnik, the self-styled Philadelphia preacher who abducted women and held them in a pre-dug pit in his basement.)

Gein, a mild-mannered, itinerant handyman from Plainfield, became everyone's nightmare when his crimes and subsequent evil doings came to public light. Gein's murder spree began on December 8, 1954, when he killed tavern owner Mary Hogan. The next year, hardware store worker Bernice Worden went missing. Bernice's son informed police that Gein was in the store the previous evening and the authorities focused their investigation on him. What they found turned the world upside down.

Bernice's body was found hanging in Gein's barn, dressed out like a deer. As bad as this was, what investigators found in the house was even more horrendous.

Amidst the filth, squalor and life's debris were bones, skin, and body parts from multiple women. Investigators learned Gein was a grave-robbing addict, exhuming corpses to employ body parts in his secret life of necrophilia.

Among the items found in the house were skulls on bedposts, four lips, and bowls made from human skulls. Horrified investigators also located Mary Hogan's face and Bernice Worden's head, masks, and leggings made from human skin, plus more. In fact, they learned Gein would don skin costumes and go out naked into his yard at night.

Gein's mother, Augusta, was a shrill, raging Christian woman, dedicated to an extreme version of the bible, and offered Ed little solace upon growing up. Upon her death, he placed her body in her pristine bedroom, where it stayed until mummified. The rest of the house was mired in unimaginable filth, including the aforementioned "trophies" of his perverse other life.

Gein was found not guilty by reason of mental disease or defect and was committed to the state's maximum security ward in Waupun for life. Some authorities opine that Gein could very well have been a pre-surgical transgender, a woman ensnared in a man's body.

Richard Macek

Macek, known as the "Baby-Face Killer" or the "Mad Biter," was convicted of murdering women in Wisconsin and Illinois. He cornered hotel maid Paula Cupit, in a Fontana, Wisconsin, room in 1974. Macek pummeled her and then stabbed her to death. He mutilated her corpse, including biting her flesh.

Macek later attempted the same behaviors with a second maid, but she survived his attacks. He returned to his native state of Illinois, where he murdered twenty-six-year-old Nancy Loosman and her three-year-old daughter. Finally, Macek attacked a woman in a laundromat, leaving her for dead in a small Illinois town. He was arrested in California and returned to Wisconsin, where he was institutionalized before dying in 1984.

Edward Edwards

Although Edwards officially murdered only two victims in Wisconsin, Tim Hack and Kelly Drew, his road map of death is long and filled with corpses. Edwards, a bombastic, self-aggrandizing, attention seeker, laid claim or did not dispute a connection to virtually every murder from the Black Dahlia to the Zodiac to Jon Benet Ramsey.

He had a deep fascination with true detective-type magazines and newspaper murder reports, and attempted to ingratiate himself into investigations. (Retired detective John Cameron wrote a book entitled *It's Me: The Serial Killer You Never Heard Of*, attempting to link Edwards to the above crimes and many more. The veracity of both the book as well as Edwards's claims have been challenged by others in the law enforcement community as nonsense.) One investigator on the Hack/Drew case offered that Edwards could have been the Zodiac killer. There was a similarity in the facial structure and Edwards traveled extensively.

From 1971-73, Edwards toured the United States as a motivational speaker on prison reform and published a book on his rehabilitation entitled *The Metamorphosis of a Criminal: The True Life Story of Ed Edwards*. Forever pushing the theory of his personal rehabilitation, Edwards appeared on such television shows as *To Tell the Truth* and *What's My Line?* while continuing his killing avocation.

Edwards is known to have murdered at least five persons including his son, but is a suspect in many other killings across the United States. Edwards died in on Ohio prison in 2011.

Robert Wirth

Wirth was a ruthless plague during the late 1980s in Milwaukee, striking a select group of citizenry: the elderly. This cowardly burglar was somewhat of an anomaly in the world of serial killers by virtue of his victim pool. Wirth targeted elderly women in their homes. (Early in the study of serial killers, it was found that younger black males would often cross color lines and target elderly white women when selecting victims. Wirth was white.)

For a brief period in 1988, Milwaukee experienced someone murdering elderly women at the rate of one per week. The murder scenes of three women matched exactly the scenes of non-lethal area burglaries with the same type of entry, as well as a chaotic trashing of the home. The victims were stabbed, beaten, and asphyxiated. Damage to the neck and voice box was brutal, most likely caused by stomping.

The homicides were linked to Wirth through DNA left at one scene and matching it to Wirth's DNA from an attempted armed robbery. He was convicted and sentenced to four consecutive life terms. He is suspected in six to eight additional murders.

Steve Daniels

Larry Hall

Known to some as the "Civil War Re-enactor" serial killer, Hall is like a malignant ghost of the Union army, a human wraith from a time long ago, still haunting the battlefields. Only this time he is not hunting Confederate soldiers, but rather unsuspecting women. The alleged serial killer traversed the Midwest in search of war re-enactments, car shows, and prey.

Hall is serving a lengthy sentence in the federal prison system for the 1983 kidnapping of an Illinois girl, fifteen-year-old Jessica Roach. Jessica was riding her bike near the Indiana border when she was abducted. Hall was arrested after Jessica's remains were found in a cornfield in Indiana. The cause of death was determined to be strangulation by object. Hall's neighbor, Chris Martin, penned a book about Hall entitled *Urges*, where he outlines his theory of the possibility Hall murdered as many as forty women.

The most famous Wisconsin case linked to Hall is the 1992 abduction of Laurie Depies in the Fox River Valley, near Menasha. Hall admitted to abducting and killing Depies, and then later reneged. He originally laid out a scenario of stalking, confronting, lying to, and then forcing her into his van. He then, according to authorities, "whisked her away from the scene, killed her, and disposed of her body."

In 1995, Wisconsin authorities were brought to a large storage room in Illinois which was utilized to house items seized by the FBI in a search of Hall's house. To the chagrin of the local investigators, it was "filled with clothes from floor to ceiling—women's clothing, girl's clothing. It was everything from undergarments to pants, to shirts, to shoes, to purses." Certainly indicative of some nefarious actions on Hall's part.

In 1993, Tricia Reitler, a nineteen-year-old who was taking a term paper break at Indiana Wesleyan University, was heading to a local neighborhood market for a can of soda when she disappeared. Later, her clothes were found near the market. Hall was arrested a year later, hovering in the vicinity. In his van were a rope, mask, and newspaper articles about the Reitler's abduction. He confessed to the killing, but later released as law enforcement authorities felt he lacked credibility.

The true number of Hall's victims will never be known unless he decides to give up the dead.

David Spanbauer

Spanbauer, who died in prison in 2002, was a nicotine-addled, wheezing, brown-fingered, "try"sexual. He did not focus his sexual fantasies and desires on a particular victim-type, rather taking advantage of whomever was in his sights and locale.

This sex offender has a long history of scoping residences in neighborhoods, and then selecting and breaking into homes of unsuspecting women to fondle, degrade, and rape. Most of the victims were adult women, but his methods and victim pool abruptly changed in 1992. He switched from attacking adult women in their homes to abducting little girls in open spaces and during daylight.

In 1992, Spanbauer abducted ten-year-old Ronelle Eichstadt near Ripon while she was riding her bike. He took her to a chosen spot, raped her, and dumped her body in a remote area.

He struck again in 1994. This time the victim was

twelve-year-old Cora Jones from Waupaca, who was riding her bike on a rural road. Cora was raped, murdered, and again Spanbauer tossed the body in a wooded area.

Spanbauer then returned to his earlier hunting behavior. In 1994, he broke into the home of twenty-one-year-old Trudi Jeschke in Appleton. While Trudi was lying on her bed talking to her boyfriend on the phone, Spanbauer crept into her house, found her bedroom, and shot her with a small-caliber handgun.

Finally, in November 1994, Spanbauer was surveilling a potential victim's home when he was noticed by the victim's neighbor. The man gave chase, tackled him, and then turned Spanbauer over to the police. Spanbauer's killing career was over.

The judge closed the sentencing proceedings by calling Spanbauer "pure evil, slithering forth from the cesspool of hell."

Alvin Taylor

Taylor and Zamastil are two of Wisconsin's little-known serial killers. Taylor was active in the central part of the state from 1985-87. He was an itinerant, out-of-work jazz musician, moving from community to community, occasionally staying with his victims, who were all his friends. The murders usually revolved around money, and it appears the active fantasy life of most serial killers was absent in Taylor's internal makeup. His killings appeared to be financially driven.

Three of Taylor's four victims were shot to death: Robert Williams, Daniel Lundgren, and Tim Haden. The fourth victim, James Severson, was stabbed. Taylor was arrested while attending Haden's funeral and later confessed to the other murders.

Taylor was delusional and found incompetent to stand trial. He was remanded to the state's mental health facility, where he remains to this day. He has petitioned the court for release on multiple occasions, but was found to remain a danger to others and is believed would most likely kill again. (Note: This is probably accurate, as many professionals have offered opinions that multiple murderers should never be released for public safety reasons.)

Walter Ellis

Ellis was a non-descript denizen of the seamy underbelly of Milwaukee's inner city. This hunter of homeless, addicted, vulnerable African-American females was dubbed "The North Side Strangler" by the press. This sobriquet fit him well as he skulked around dirty, dilapidated areas of the city looking for victims to rape and murder. This area of the city was his comfort zone, and he used it to great advantage for over twenty years.

By most accounts, his killings spanned 1986-2007. Ellis had been arrested numerous times prior to his capture for the serial killings, including for attacking a woman with a hammer in 1998. He was convicted of killing seven women: Deborah Harris, Tanya Miller, Irene Smith, Florence McCormack, Sheila Farrior, Joyce Mims, and Quithreaun Stokes. He died in prison in 2013 of natural causes.

Jeffrey Dahmer

Dahmer, the well-known cannibal of Milwaukee, turned the criminal justice world on its head with the sheer depravity of his crimes, much like Ed Gein did forty years earlier.

Dahmer's killings actually began when he was eighteen years old. Left alone at his home in Ohio while his father was away on business, he picked up a hitchhiker, Steven Hicks. When Hicks attempted to leave, Dahmer killed him, burying his body in the back yard. There was a break in the killings for nine years before Dahmer's killings became an addiction, much like his drinking. In fact, in a prison interview, he labeled his killings as just that, an addiction.

Dahmer relocated to Milwaukee and the killing began anew. He simply transplanted his sexual perversity to a new locale. While in Milwaukee, Dahmer exposed himself to an unwitting victim, and for this transgression was placed on probation. It was soon after that his hunting – seducing, drugging, and killing homosexual men – took on a life of its own.

Dahmer would troll gay bars, nightclubs, malls, and bus stations, and upon identifying his victim, the wooing would begin. Dahmer would dance, drink, hug, and whisper sweet nothings into a potential victim's ear. He would compliment them profusely, suggesting he would like to photograph them. He brought them to his apartment, which was beginning to take on the aura of a slaughter house.

This killer would drug the unsuspecting victim and then murder him, taking pornographic photos. After killing his prey using various methods, he would flay, dissect, and mutilate the corpse. He would cut bodies into bits in an effort to dispose of them by flushing them down the toilet. Like Shakespearean witches with their burbling black pot of evil hexes, Dahmer also kept a cauldron of caustic goo to melt the remaining body parts.

Dahmer's trophies consisted of heads, sexual organs, skinned hands, and penises kept in the freezer. He had painted skulls, attempting to build a haphazard altar in his living room, and had portions of bodies stacked in the tub. These bodies had despicable behaviors inflicted upon them, ranging from organs removed to items inserted in the rectal cavity, and showed signs of cannibalism.

Dahmer admitted to having killed fifteen to seventeen victims and was sentenced to fifteen life sentences. On November 28, 1994, Dahmer's lifeless body was found in a pool of blood in a prison restroom. Next to him was a bloodied broom handle. He had been bludgeoned to death by another inmate, Chris Scarver.

On a related note: Tracy Edwards was the only potential victim of Dahmer's to escape. He then led police to the killer's lair. Edwards was later charged with murder in the death of a homeless man, throwing the man off a bridge in Milwaukee. Almost twenty years to the day later, July 26, 2011, the once-almost victim became the victimizer.

Edwards's life spiraled out of control shortly after the Dahmer debacle. He was often homeless, wandering from shelter to shelter or living on the streets. Prior to his murder charge, he was extradited to Mississippi to face one count of molesting a fourteen-year-old girl. He often engaged in minor crimes, falling into the morass of drugs, ill health, and general malaise.

Nancy Moronez

On February 28, 2018, a sixty-year-old Oshkosh woman was charged with the murder of three infant children, including her son, which occurred over a period of time in the 1980s. If convicted (the case was still in progress at the time of this writing), her cases would emphasize that men do not have sole claim to the term serial killer.

Moronez is charged with killing three infants starting with Justin Brunka, her son, in 1980. She went on to allegedly kill Brad Steege in 1984. Lastly, she was charged with the murder of Katie Kozeniecki in 1985. All babies appear to have been killed by suffocation or drowning. According to her statements to police, she simply could not tolerate the babies' crying.

William Zamastil

It is believed Zamastil began and ended his killing persona in Wisconsin, and between these endpoints, traversed the country seeking to satisfy his unending bloodlust. He murdered because hunting his victims was fun, and he would discuss his killings as "offing people." He was the Grim Reaper to many unsuspecting victims.

Although one of his murders is discussed in the first chapter of this book, Zamastil's crimes, profile, and prison life will be addressed in more detail in the following chapters.

Other serial killers with Wisconsin ties (and the number of victims):
- Lorenzo Faye (6)
- James Duquette, Jr. (2+)
- Lawrence Dalton (4)
- Kim Brown (3)
- Michael Herrington (2+)
- Michael Tenneson (5)
- Joseph Franklin (20)
- David Van Dyke (6+)
- Alton Coleman and Debra Brown (8)

There are numerous investigators who believe that Henry Lucas and Ottis Toole, a pair of marauding sex deviates, murdered some of their victims in Wisconsin. Numbers are uncertain. While Toole was on death row in Florida, Ted Bundy, another condemned serial killer, offered that Toole didn't have the IQ of whipped cream.

An interesting case with Wisconsin ties is that of Randall Woodfield. After dropping out of Portland State University in 1974, Woodfield was drafted by the Green Bay Packers with the 428th pick. Woodfield returned to Oregon after being cut by the team and began a murderous career, earning the title "The I-5 Killer." He engaged in sexual assaults and armed robberies, and is linked to eighteen murders.

Lastly is the bizarre and much-maligned theory posited by two retired New York City detectives of a gang of serial killers known as the "Smiley Face Killers" roaming the college campuses of Wisconsin and Minnesota, drowning unsuspecting college males in waterways close to the city bars and campuses. These two investigators offer that there could be as many as forty victims, all male, mostly white, and probably highly intoxicated. The killers' calling cards are smiley faces drawn nearby the drowning spots.

Most detectives in the locales where the mishap/crimes occur seriously downplay the theory, indicating the drownings are no more than inebriated young men losing their bearings after a night of heavy drinking, and falling prey to nothing more than losing footing in nearby bodies of water. Many of the parents still demand further investigation despite town hall meetings held by local authorities and an inquiry by the FBI which turned up no evidence of foul play or a serial killer.

"If you ain't dead, I ain't interested."

- *Retired homicide investigator's screensaver*

Chapter 4

The Player in the Hunt

William Zamastil is a serial killer, Wisconsin born and bred. He is not as well-known as his Wisconsin "brethren," but possibly no less prolific. In fact, he may be even more so if suspected murders are added into the equation.

In order to know William Zamastil, you need to meet someone ...

Steve Daniels

Special Agent Rick Luell
Wisconsin Department of Justice

Special Agent Luell is a man who is no stranger to high-profile homicide cases. Luell offered a brief personal history for this work, touching on a few murders in his "portfolio of mayhem."

Luell was the founder and first president of the Wisconsin Association of Homicide Investigators. He was also a three-time recipient of that association's Michael Vendola Death Investigator of the Year Award. He, and other members of the Leesa Jo Shaner investigation team, were awarded a prestigious honor by the International Homicide Investigator's Association. Luell retired prior to his involvement in the Zamastil case, but returned to service as the result of a cold case grant.

Another investigator who aided in bringing Zamastil to justice was the late Ed Gorski, Chief Deputy in the Sauk County Sheriff's Department. Gorski was instrumental in dealing with Zamastil in the investigation of the Mary Johnson killing. In fact, once Zamastil was in custody in Wisconsin, Gorski became the focal point for other investigations potentially involving Zamastil. Gorski answered requests from out-of-area agencies, served on task forces, and aided in investigations. This dedicated and dogged investigator spent countless hours hunting perpetrators, earning the nickname J. Edgar (after the former FBI director).

There were certainly other investigators in and out of Zamastil's murderous life, but some are deceased, some are retired, and some simply didn't want to be a part of this publication.

The Tim Haack and Kelly Drew murders
August 9, 1980

Sweethearts Tim Hack and Kelly Drew were a farm couple-to-be headed to a wedding reception in Jefferson, Wisconsin, on a sweltering summer night. After meeting friends, the couple decided to ditch the reception and head to a local carnival. They never made it, nor did they return to their respective homes that night. Authorities launched a massive search, the largest in Wisconsin history at the time. One early theory was the pair were victims of prolific wandering killer, Henry Lucas.

Drew's car was found in a ditch near the side of a rural road. Some ominous items were located in a separate area suggesting foul play had occurred, including Kelly's pants slit from ankle to crotch, a chunk of rope, and a hunk of yellow tubing. Approximately one month later, both bodies were located in near proximity to each other. Kelly had been sexually assaulted. They were together in life and together in death.

Agent Luell worked closely with Detective Chad Garcia, who was working on this double murder as a cold case. The aforementioned serial killer Edward Edwards was convicted of the murders as part of a cold case investigation, and a long-open case was closed.

Steve Daniels

The Michael Madden murder
June 27, 1990

Michael Madden was a door-to-door fundraiser in the Racine area for Wisconsin Citizens for a Better Environment. Mike stopped at a house in rural Racine County while engaged in his job on the above date. The house, owned by Joachim Dressler, was next to a church, but would become Mike's gateway to hell. He was invited into the house of horrors by Dressler with hopes of scoring a donation. Instead, he met Satan.

From this point, theories are a bit murky. One school of thought suggests that because Dressler's family was not at home, he attempted to enter into a homosexual relationship with the victim and was rebuffed. Another theory offers that Dressler was so addicted to "murder porn," that he was driven to act out on the addiction.

No one will know for certain, but what is fact is that Dressler murdered Madden and then dismembered his body. Dressler placed Mike's torso, legs, arms, and pelvis into separate bags, and then dumped them in scattered locales. Investigators found videos of what appeared to be actual torture, mutilation, and murder in the Dressler home, along with a cache of photos of dead people.

Dressler was convicted and sentenced to life in prison.

The Darlene Egan murder
August 22, 1990

Dan and Darlene Egan resided in Green Lake County in central Wisconsin, where they were embroiled in a nasty divorce and child custody battle. On the day after the final divorce decree, the couple was riding together in the same vehicle, with Darlene driving. According to Dan, Darlene swerved in an effort to miss a deer in the road and crashing into a water-filled ditch. Dan stated to authorities that he attempted to assist Darlene, but was not successful. He then left the vehicle to obtain help.

Green Lake County authorities originally attributed Darlene's death to accidental drowning and thought to close the case. However, during the autopsy, the medical examiner found marks on Darlene's head indicating her head had been held under water. A criminal investigation ensued, culminating in the conviction of Dan Egan for first degree intentional homicide.

In the course of this investigation, Agent Luell was assigned the task of investigating the cold case homicide of the bludgeoning death of an elderly woman, also in Green Lake County.

Luell Meets an Informant

As was standard operating procedure for Agent Luell, he visited various prisons to interview inmates incarcerated from counties in which he had active investigations. This practice often gave him access to quality information. It was in this manner he met a particular inmate and the unraveling of William Zamastil's murderous existence began.

The inmate himself was incarcerated on a life sentence for first degree murder. And even though he became a main informant with a deep well of information on Zamastil, his integrity was in question as a result of his rather shady background. The inmate completely enjoyed the limelight that his Zamastil information allowed him to enjoy. He was, in crime parlance, a "leg man" in an organized crime pornography ring. The lure of money, as well as the excitement of evading the police, were great motivators for this felon. In an effort to occasionally extricate himself from this path of crime, the inmate would vacation in Green Lake County, a rural tourist area.

He informed Agent Luell that he did not have any pertinent information on Luell's Green Lake County cases, but he was in contact with another inmate who was bragging and offering insight into murders in Wisconsin as well as out west.

Enter William Zamastil

The inmate told Luell that he met Zamastil when they had been incarcerated together in 1984-85 at the maximum security institution in Waupun, Wisconsin. They were also cellmates for four years at a less-restrictive institution later on. He mentioned on multiple occasions

Gazing Into the Abyss

that, "Bill's a good guy, a solid con, but a piece of shit human."

According to the inmate, Zamastil wanted to "get tight" with the Outlaws motorcycle club. Since the inmate was friendly with biker types, Zamastil thought his jailhouse friend might be an in. Zamastil also figured his buddy would never get released because of the nature of his crime, and began telling the man about his victims. Zamastil became even more willing to talk after receiving a four-year defer from the parole board.

(A four-year defer is when the parole board says they will not see the inmate for four more years. It should be noted that Zamastil will never be released as there is a detainer on him from the federal system. This detainer would automatically transfer him to the federal prison system should he obtain a parole from Wisconsin. The parole board has seen Zamastil numerous times with what appears to be no interest in releasing him. He has not completed necessary treatment programs.)

When Zamastil began telling his inmate friend about his "kills," his fellow con proffered that he was going to tell the authorities.

Zamastil offered that his first victim was named Christine, and that he was fifteen or sixteen when he committed the murder. He stated he joined the army after that. (The murder of Christine Rothschild occurred in Madison, Wisconsin, in 1968 and to this day remains unsolved.)

In the inimitable inmate fashion, Zamastil continued to discuss his murders. He bragged that he "offed a cop's son out west." He also went into great detail about his role in the murder of a sister and brother who were hitchhiking in California.

The inmate told Agent Luell that he felt Zamastil was a serial killer with possibly fourteen or more victims. He said bodies were piled up in the southwestern United States as well as California. Zamastil suggested that he would bury bodies in mine shafts in areas that looked as though they were post-apocalyptic.

Chuckling that there was never a dull moment will Zamastil, the inmate said Zamastil relished discussing his crimes, enjoyed killing, and loved the hunt. He was like a praying mantis, awaiting the right moment to pounce on an unsuspecting victim. His antennae went up, he looked around, and bam! A correctional officer assigned to a cellblock that housed Zamastil stated the killer would get up every morning to the mantra of, "I long for the taste of blood."

The inmate became an invaluable source of information for Special Agent Luell, corresponding and meeting with him on numerous occasions. He was also flown out west, while still incarcerated, to testify in a murder trial against Zamastil. During one session, he testified for two hours.

The informant currently is on parole supervision in northern Wisconsin, living with his wife.

"Murderers are not monsters, they are men. And that is the most frightening thing about them."

- Author Alice Sebold

Chapter 5

Who the Hell is William Zamastil?

Forensic psychiatrist Dr. Helen Morrison offers that serial murderers tend toward a "cookie-cutter syndrome," with backgrounds featuring striking similarities. They tend to be hypochondriacs, chatty, remorseless men who are addicted to the most brutal acts – stabbings, strangulation, rape – and see their victims as inanimate objects.

Dr. Morrison was quoted as saying, "You say to yourself, 'How could anybody do this to another human being?' Then you realize they don't see them as humans. To the killer, it's like pulling the wings off a fly or the legs off of a daddy long legs. You just want to see what happens."

Many killers, in an effort to dehumanize their victims, do not call them by anything remotely human. Often they use the phrase "my crime" or "my case," or like BTK killer Dennis Rader called his murders, "my projects." They might say, "I killed the bitch!" Ted Bundy said, "It was like changing a tire." Zamastil said it was like hunting. These killers simply do not see their victims as anything close to a person.

This author attempted contact with William Zamastil for this publication, so this portion will be presented in a case study format.

Early Years

William Zamastil was born on May 17, 1952, at St. Mary's Hospital in Madison, Wisconsin, to Mr. and Mrs. Chester Zamastil. He has three older siblings and two younger brothers. Growing up, he resided in the Madison suburb of Middleton, within a family unit described as stable. He ran away from home on numerous occasions about the age of fifteen, which necessitated placement in a juvenile mental health facility for evaluations. There is some debate whether he was in Mendota State Hospital or the old University Hospital, which was located across the street from Sterling Hall, where Christine Rothschild's body was found at that time in 1968. Both facilities had inpatient psychiatric units, and if Zamastil was at the now-defunct University of Wisconsin site, it would have given him a vantage point from which to watch Ms. Rothschild on her walks.

Zamastil offered that he garnered mediocre grades in school with little effort, but completed only ninth grade. There is no indication of any history of MacDonald triad issues: bed-wetting, fire starting, or abuse of animals. Zamastil had attempted suicide on more than one occasion, according to his sister.

He enlisted in the United States Army in 1971 at age nineteen, receiving a general discharge with honorable conditions. There is documentation that he went absent without leave (AWOL) in 1969.

Zamastil was married and divorced twice. He has one known child, a daughter. In a May 7, 2013, institution report, he refused to name a next of kin.

Criminal History (early)

12/30/1971 – Operating a motor vehicle without owner's consent. Two years' probation to the Wisconsin Department of Social Services. (Now Department of Corrections)

8/1971 – Stole another vehicle, used the owner's credit card, and then returned the vehicle. Probation revoked, sixty days in jail.

5/11/1971 – Petty theft, twenty-one days in the county jail.

8/15/1974 – Grand theft, sentence withheld, placed on sixteen months' probation and restitution ordered. Offender absconded, probation was revoked.

11/26/1974 – Sentenced to one year in jail.

2/17/1975 – Petty theft, San Bernardino, California. Sixty days in jail. This seems to be the catalyst for Zamastil's murders out west, but due to the paucity of information on this offender's behavioral history, it is difficult to determine which life event actually moved him on his murderous path.

8/1/1978 – Sauk County, Wisconsin. First degree murder, sexual assault. Life sentence, plus twenty years.

Incarceration Time

Zamastil is currently in maximum security at Waupun Correctional Institution (Wisconsin). He has detainers on him from California for two homicides and a federal detainer from Arizona, also for a homicide.

According to internal Wisconsin Department of Corrections documentation, Zamastil is in need of sex offender programming, along with alcohol and drug treatment. He is not thought to have any physical defects or genetic abnormalities; however, his attorney suggested he has a serious personality disorder exacerbated by alcohol. He is considered a high-risk inmate, and release would pose a great risk to the community. The detainers on him from two other states makes his release a moot point. He would immediately be held and transported to another jurisdiction to begin that particular sentence.

When asked by prison staff to discuss the murder of Mary Johnson, which is part of the Re-Classification Report, he blurted "no need to rehash." It appears it is easier for him to brag to inmates about his murders rather than discussing the killing of Ms. Johnson in a rational, therapeutic way.

Zamastil's institutional behavior can be considered belligerent at best. Thumbing through random conduct reports, there are a number of them that are worrisome, including ten for threats and a number for disrespect and disobeying orders. Many of the threats, as indicated on conduct reports, are bombastic name-calling and spontaneous idle threats as result of lack of temper control or a sense of being dismissed. Staff are called bitches, pussies and punks. Two California-based investigators were called faggots. The results of these outbursts are usually loss of privileges or time in segregation.

Three of the conduct reports studied seem rather egregious:

On 3/29/1979, there was a fight in a cellblock between Zamastil and another inmate. Zamastil, apparently the aggressor, had his foe in a headlock, pushing his head and neck into the door jamb. He also attempted to strangle the other inmate.

The second occurred on 3/25/1987. According to the conduct report, Zamastil intimidated and threatened to kill other inmates if they refused to abet in violating institution rules and policies. Zamastil told one inmate, "If we were someplace else, I'd already killed you by now." He made these threats in the presence of other inmates. The victimized inmates felt that Zamastil and his cronies would either physically or sexually assault them.

The other disturbing behavior involved a euphemistically named inmate group called the European Culture Group. (Many criminal justice professionals would consider this a prison-based, white-supremacist front group). On 3/18/1989, again at Waupun, the afore-mentioned group was holding its banquet, including inmates as well as numerous outside guests. At one point in the festivities, about twenty inmates, including Zamastil, left their guests and gathered in the center of the banquet locale. This, according to the conduct report, was a meeting of the Prison Motorcycle Brotherhood, an unsanctioned group. (Read gang). This put a damper on the rest of the evening and served as a show of power by this gang.

Profile of Zamastil

A profile of this offender is a behavioral portrait sketched from physicality, actions, and crime-related actions.

Personal/Behavioral

• A talented mechanic who was sporadically employed out west. He lived in Barstow and Needles, California.

• He often lived a vagabond, nomadic lifestyle, hitchhiking from location to location.

• He was extremely chameleon-like, often presenting himself as a nice guy.

• He claims to have criminal records in multiple states. (This certainly is true with his murders.)

• He had a very short "killing career," with his first murder possibly as a teenager and his last in his early twenties.

• In an odd twist: a registered sex offender named Mark Harris reportedly used William Zamastil as an alias.

- An episodic killer appearing as a hulking, ogre-like man standing six-feet-four, weighing in at 290 pounds with a shaved head, replete with a dragon skull tattoo.
- A macho man-type who gorges on various types of cookies, often Girl Scout Cookies.
- Occasionally easy-going, but can be riled easily; arrogant, and a bully to other inmates. Said to have a Jekyll/Hyde personality.
- Believes if other inmates were aware of his multiple killings, they would be intimidated. One correctional officer stated that he was a "snitch."
- According to a relative, he is bisexual when he needs a place to stay or desires something from someone. She offered that "at one time, Bill worked in a hotel in downtown LA, where he was probably living with a homosexual."
- His sister offered she was not surprised that her brother might be implicated in numerous killings, stating "he has the attitude and is capable."
- Chronic gambler. Loves to play poker.
- Braggart
- Lacks self-confidence
- Manipulator
- Enjoys taunting the police

Crime-Related

- His killing methods varied from bludgeoning to strangling to shooting.
- Female victims were sexually assaulted, most were robbed. One male victim was sexually assaulted. Victims were left unclothed.

- Took trinkets or property from his victims. (Suitcase, ring and wallet, and a set of keys). These are called souvenirs in the lexicon of behavioral analysis.)
- Stone sober during the killings (according to inmate informant). However, he had been drinking prior to murdering Mary Johnson and admitted to drinking often. Said other than the murder of Ms. Johnson, he had a reason to kill. It appears his motivation was sexual desire and the thrill of the hunt.
- Always wore either cowboy or engineer boots, according to a relative. Boot prints were found at numerous crime scenes. One suspected victim told her sister she was "traveling with a cowboy."
- Was remorseless. Said he killed when the need arose. A profile of this killer says "he is cold-blooded, evil, loves power, and is totally turned over to the dark side." According to the jailhouse informant, Zamastil has eerie eyes, no regrets, and the famous thousand-yard stare.
- Always carried a knife.
- Violent temper.
- Enjoyed killing. Zamastil offered, "If you like to hunt, it's the thrill of the hunt."
- Abducted victims in populated places (mall parking lot, or airport car ramp. Side of a highway.) Victims of convenience.
- Dumped bodies in rural, isolated places. Body disposal sites were haphazard, with apparently little planning. Some were surface burials, such as barely covered with leaves and/or debris. Some were dumped in abandoned mine shafts. In fact, Zamastil was a drifter who

roamed around and through the Mojave Desert, which is considered the number one body dump site in the United States.

- Haphazard use of forensic countermeasures. (These are actions taken by the offender in an effort to thwart law enforcement.) Again, his victim burials were of convenience with no planning aforethought. In fact, he left his wallet at the crime scene of his last murder and the victim's body in plain view, unburied. (Staging a crime scene, such as trashing the room to look as if something had been taken to throw off investigators, is a common forensic countermeasure used by select killers. If the scene is manipulated for the sole purpose of sexual gratification of the offender, such as spreading the victim's legs, this is known as posing.)
- Risk taker
- Primarily chose low-risk victims. (Low-risk victims are those individuals engaged in regular activities that do not usually put them in harm's way. Zamastil abducted a woman leaving work and a woman picking up her husband at an airport. He picked up siblings hitchhiking, which is usually a high-risk behavior, but this was a pair, not a single victim that would have been easier to control. High-risk victims are drug addicts, homeless individuals, runaways, etc.
- Traveled extensively. (He told a sister there were only two states he had not been in.)

Summarizing Zamastil as a Killer

1. He used various weapons and kill methods.

2. He chose various victims, both men and women. There was no consistency in his victim pool. (A victim pool is the grouping of specific victims for many killers, such as hitchhikers, drug addicts, prostitutes, elderly, or children. A certain physical feature, such as blonde hair, or a disability might be part of the attraction. One serial offender in the Midwest targeted handicapped individuals living in special needs facilities. Their choices are made to suit their predatory tastes. Many killers do not stray from their chosen pool.)

3. He was an extremely mobile killer, traversing the country in search of victims.

4. He was a disorganized killer, often acting spontaneously with no pre-planning. There was a modicum of organized traits, such as bringing a weapon (a gun) to his crimes. He also left few, if any, witnesses.

Because Zamastil refused to discuss himself or his past crimes, there is a scarcity of information on this particular killer's earlier life. It appears he often flew under the radar, like a vole in a backyard or a submarine below the surface, until his final murder in 1978. When incarcerated in Wisconsin, his past began to catch up with him, leading a multiplicity of investigators to his door in an effort to sort out numerous killings over multiple jurisdictions.

"A man lusts to become a god ... and there is murder. Murder upon murder, upon murder. Why is the world of men nothing but murder?"

- Author David Zindell

Chapter 6

Christine: Was She the First Victim?

The murder of Christine Rothschild is strange, sad, and unsolved. To many, including the University of Wisconsin Police Department, the slaying of this young woman is a riddle, encased in an enigma, entombed in a conundrum.

The case unfolds as follows:

On May 26, 1968, a vivacious, comely, and petite young woman donned the student attire of the day: a mini-skirt and go-go boots. She grabbed a coat to begin her regular early-morning jaunt across campus. But this cold, blustery, and bleak spring morning would be different. Christine Rothschild's walk from her dorm would be her demise. She was murdered, and her body stashed behind bushes by Sterling Hall on the university campus. (This hall gained even more notoriety in the early 1970s when a rag-tag bunch of anti-war radicals bombed the hall, killing an Army math researcher.)

Christine was a young woman looking toward the future. She enjoyed campus life, developed friendships, and seemed to have things in order; except, according to her best friend, Linda Shulko, Christine had an ominous feeling of being followed, "spied on," and watched.

After years of personal research, investigating, and tracking, Shulko purported that the person who murdered her friend was a heretofore unknown serial killer she identified as Dr. Niels Jorgensen, a physician of ill repute who by some accounts had murdered his own brother. Handsome, arrogant, and downright creepy, Jorgensen was specter-like. He seemed to appear out of nowhere and cast a pall on those in contact with him. Jorgensen dressed in camouflage and wallowed in the grisly images of machete-hacked families purported to be in other countries. They were very likely murdered by the doctor himself.

Dr. Michael Arntfield, in his well-written book *Mad City: The True Story of the Campus Murders That America Forgot*, posits that Jorgensen was, in fact, the slayer of Christine Rothschild. Arntfield lays out a case complete with crime scene specifics so detailed it appears he could have been present when the body was found. Arntfield describes the finding of Christine's body by a student worker and the ghastly crime scene in the following way:

The scene was a "grotesque tableau that had been carefully arranged to provide a very specific message once found. Christine had been intricately posed on her back with her head resting on the cement ledge of the foundation window. Beneath her bloodied head was a 'calling card,' an expensive, classy man's cotton handkerchief."

Arntfield believes the memento was left there as an in-your-face gesture for investigators as well as part of the killer's elaborate fantasy. It provided a mind picture that assisted the killer in reliving Christine's murder.

Continuing with the crime scene narration, Arntfield writes, "Christine's head was turned to the side and ravaged, both sides of her jaw were shattered and her head pulverized." She was most likely knocked out by an initial blow. He paints a bloody still-life scene of horror, writing, "Christine's blue shift dress was matted with red crimson and gore; it was later confirmed that her torso had been pierced a total of fourteen times with some comparatively obscure type of finely sharpened weapon, later described as some type of medical weapon ... a scalpel."

It was later ascertained that there were many more indignities done to Christine in what appears to be a frenzied display of the killer's fantasy life. Arntfield writes, "Christine's boots had been removed by the killer and then placed back on the body after her textured panty hose were removed and taken as a souvenir. Christine's beige, quilted trench coat was still on her body, with the interior lining torn out, to be used as a garrote after she was apparently already dead."

It was suggested this was done as an act of control by the killer, as well as "a paraphilic boasting of numerous twisted fetishes, one of which would seem to be necrophilia, which involves sexually motivated interference, posing, and ravaging the body after death." Arntfield also suggested that the elaborate tourniquet might have served another purpose: that being to delay recovery from Christine's throat of her "tan sheepskin dress gloves ... both inserted postmortem."

What is extremely interesting about this murder are the number of items taken from the victim in order to "rewind and replay the whole scene as a type of brain movie in the future whenever he (Jorgensen) held or gazed upon the souvenirs of his work." Pilfered from Christine's corpse were her "pantyhose. He also took blue Sunday ribbon from hair, and the brass lighter from the right pocket of her trench coat, but left behind money and jewelry." (Arntfield writes that "the bow and pantyhose would have to be part of his private collection, the lighter could be hidden in plain sight, used in day-to-day functioning.")

Arntfield offers a remaining crime scene oddity that "reappeared in at least this crime, and numerous other murders across the country, could only have been committed by one person, Niels Jorgensen. Inserted into the grass immediately in front of Christine's feet was her designer black umbrella, in itself innocuous given the rainy weather. Rather than taking the umbrella as a twisted keepsake as he did with other items, or merely discarding it, the killer took time to elaborately set up something of a macabre diorama."

He added: "Christine's umbrella hadn't just been spear-tipped into the rain-soaked ground like some type of javelin. It had been inserted with precision at a ninety-degree angle with the handle pointed at the sky, the umbrella opened with the metal stays, either manually snapped or cut one at a time, arrayed around the entire circumference of the canopy. The umbrella itself was mutilated, just like Christine's body, to suit an aesthetic theme."

A November 2010 newspaper article in Madison's *The Capitol Times* entitled "Evidence Lost in at Least 4 Dane County Homicides" states that evidence in the Christine Rothschild murder case had "simply been lost." The University of Wisconsin Police Department's chief decided to take a fresh look at the unsolved murder and formed a task force in 2007. UWPD records were kept in the Dane County Sheriff's Department at the time due to space constraints at the university. When records were requested by the task force, some were not available. According to the article, although exact items missing were not noted, important physical evidence had been sent to the FBI for examination. There was no documentation of results received, nor that anything sent to the bureau's lab was ever returned.

The preceding descriptions of Christine Rothschild's murder, including the crime scene and fetishes of Niels Jorgensen, seem well-researched, detailed, and forensically probable, but there is one glitch in the narrative. William Zamastil has admitted on more than one occasion to the murder. The aforementioned Special Agent Luell stated the killer was ready to admit to this crime as part of a plea arrangement, but backed out.

This was verified by Zamastil's former cellmate. According to the confidential informant, Zamastil discussed an old homicide in Madison where a student was killed. Zamastil offered that this was his "first kill' when he was fifteen or sixteen, and that he joined the army afterwards.

Jeff Mathwig, a researcher at the Center for Homicide Research, offers in an unfinished paper that "Offenders themselves have spoken about their first kill explicitly, as to imply that as the first, there will be a second, third and so on." This fits Zamastil perfectly. The informant went on to state he believes the victim was a student at UW-Madison. "Her name was (K)rissy or (K)ristine Rothschild, and the murder occurred in 1968 or '69."

In what could be a snide, disrespectful aside to Christine's murder, the cellmate stated that Zamastil was going to plead to her murder in a case-related deal, but reneged because the institution he would be assigned to was not going to have "chunky peanut butter in the dining area."

Special Agent Luell offered that Zamastil wanted to continue to serve his sentence in Wisconsin as opposed to California. Contingent to this deal, Zamastil needed to plead guilty to murdering Christine Rothschild. When Luell returned from retirement to work on a backlog of cold cases, he learned that the attorney general's office had dropped the ball in the interim, allowing Zamastil to remain in his home state without pleading to killing Christine. Luell went back to Zamastil and reminded him about their agreement. Zamastil blew off the investigator and the rest is history. The murder of Christine Rothschild remains unsolved to date.

Mike Arntfield offers that as a teenager, Zamastil's paraphilia could not have been developed to the point of those demonstrated at the crime scene. He also suggests that Zamastil would not have been that sophisticated at that age. But Luell maintains that Zamastil watched Christine, dragged her down, and then shoved black leather gloves in her mouth to stop her from screaming. Luell feels it was a bumbling crime scene, a "novice attempt at sexual assault." Probably a lot of grabbing and touching, and then Zamastil lost control of the situation. According to reports, Zamastil is still considered a person of interest in the case by the UWPD, the lead agency in this case.

There are many teenage serial killers in the annals of crime. The stories of two young killers are examined below.

Craig Price

Price, described as an obese African-American, was born October 11, 1973, in Warwick, Rhode Island. He had a long history of petty crimes, including thefts. But it was crimes much more sinister, shocking, and vile that gave him the moniker "The Warwick Slasher."

It was a hot evening on July 27, 1989, when a thirteen-year-old Price entered the world of the infamous. On that date, this huge, Baby Huey-like man-child killed his first human being, twenty-seven-year-old Rebecca Spencer. The single mother of two lived but two houses down from her personal Grim Reaper. Price entered Rebecca's house and proceeded to stab her fifty-eight times.

Price's bloodlust was not sated. Two years later, as a fifteen-year-old high school freshman, Price crawled even deeper into the abyss when he murdered an entire family while high on drugs. Again he entered the home of neighbors, this time the residence of Joan Heaton (39), and her daughters Jennifer (10) and Melissa (8). Price stabbed Joan fifty-seven times and bit her face. He stabbed Jennifer sixty-two times and Melissa thirty times. Melissa was also beaten about the head with a kitchen stool.

Some wounds were so deep that the knives broke off in the victim and the killer was forced to use other weapons. A total of approximately 149 stab wounds were inflicted on the three victims. Often, with this many stab wounds, the killer is in a sexual frenzy and simply cannot stop the stabbing until his energy is spent. He could be physically sexually aroused.

There is an odd twist in this case. The local police department brought in the FBI to develop a profile of the killer. The profiler offered that as both murder scenes were virtually steps apart, the killer most likely walked to the crime scenes and lived in the area. The assumption was that whomever perpetrated these acts must be Caucasian, since the neighborhood was a mostly white, middle-class enclave.

Jorge Torrez

On Monday, July 13, 2009, Petty Officer Amanda Snell did not report for work at her naval posting near Alexandria, Virginia. Friends in her dorm were contacted to check on her welfare. Her room was military neat. To the searchers' chagrin, Amanda was found dead, her body stuffed into a locker with her head encased in a pillow cover.

As the investigation meandered its way through 2009 and into 2010, police were being confronted with home invasions, attempted abductions, and brutal sexual assaults. There was at least one attempted murder in the area. What stood out in the investigators' minds was the seeming omnipresence of a Dodge Durango in peculiar places at strange times. It was seen either in close proximity to or mentioned in relationship to the actual crimes.

After an arduous investigation, Jorge Torrez was arrested on February 27, 2010. Police located a stun gun used in one case, plus "souvenirs from a victim." In searching the killer's room, authorities located a Glock pistol, his computer with directions on using chloroform, and his pornography collection featuring rape and suffocation.

The story doesn't end there, and in fact investigators later learned it began in Zion, Illinois, when Torrez was sixteen years old. Torrez lured two little girls, eight-year-old Laura Hobbs and nine-year-old Krystal Tobias into the woods on Mother's Day, 2005, with the intent to harm the girls. Using the ploy of playing hide and seek, Torrez took Krystal deep into the woods to "hide with him," leaving Laura to find them. While waiting to be found, Torrez stabbed Krystal four times to basically get her out of the way.

Now unencumbered by a witness, Torrez attacked Laura, stabbing her twenty times. He also sexually assaulted her and mutilated her body. When the search party found the girls' bodies, both sets of shoes were arranged neatly next to them. (This could be what is known as "undoing." This behavior by the killer is an impossible attempt to undo the murder. In a flash of remorse or extreme discomfort, the killer does something "nice" for the victim, in this case arranging shoes neatly. In other instances, it could be covering the victim, doing the dishes, or wiping off the table). Later, when the girls' grandparents returned to the woods where the murders occurred, they found a chair, liquor bottle, and lubricant, all indicative of pre-planning on Torrez's part.

Questions remain

Is a teenager too young to repeatedly kill? Many experts feel Ted Bundy began killing in his teens with the murder of an eight-year-old girl from his hometown. Serial killer John Gacy is a suspect in the 1955 murder of three young boys ages 11-13. They were found in the neighborhood where Gacy lived. He would have been fifteen.

Were both Price and Torrez sophisticated enough for pre-planning? Could Zamastil have killed Christine Rothschild as he was so temporarily wanting to admit, or was Jorgensen the person who killed her?

In an odd twist of crime statistics, the Madison Police Department did not list her murder for a period of time. Since the crime occurred on the University of Wisconsin campus, it was technically on state property, not the city. Sadly, not only does the murder remain unsolved, but for a period of time, Christine Rothschild was not even considered dead in Madison.

"And I saw a beast rising out of the sea ..."

- **Revelation 13:1**

Chapter 7

Zamastil's Other Known and Suspected Victims

William Zamastil does not rank as a prolific serial killer in the annals of episodic death by many standards. In fact, based on the number of actual convictions, this man probably resides on the third or fourth rung of the "ladder of serial killers." Many readers will probably count him as a lesser player on the stage of serial violence. One professional offered that Zamastil "is not a heavy hitter like others."

In Dante's *Inferno*, Zamastil might be in the lesser level of hell, not on level nine, which is considered the deepest, most extreme level where Satan himself dwells. This level is void of all sources of light and warmth, and most likely houses the likes of Ted Bundy, John Gacy, Leonard Lake, David Parker, and Richard Ramirez among others. (Ramirez, an avowed Satanist, would probably feel right at home.) To others, particularly the survivors and loved ones of his numerous victims, Zamastil is a bizarre fungus that infected their lives and turned their world into a dark nightmare.

Zamastil's victim count could be considered high in terms of being viewed as a person of interest or a suspect. Police files are replete with scores of faceless men and women murdered. Bodies were located near him, around him, and in his wake during the time this convicted killer roamed the western United States. He was a scourge on society, a potential one-man killing machine. Zamastil "scores" a 21 on an unscientific Depravity Point Scale that is listed on a murder-related blog. This scale addresses aggravating circumstances surrounding the offender's crimes such as multiple murders, sexual assaults, abductions, and method of operation.

A memorandum written in May 1979 by a law enforcement agency in Arizona, one year after Zamastil was arrested for his final homicide, indicates that a task force was looking into at least twenty homicides attributed to this killer. Fifteen separate agencies were attempting to cull their information for a coordinated meeting to be held in Las Vegas. A main focus of this conference was to develop "Zamastil's background, methods of operation (MO), motives, and personality."

A separate document authored by a San Francisco Police Department captain, dated July 1979, discusses the fact that Zamastil was in that area until October 24, 1979. The letter goes on to suggest this killer might be willing to discuss "alleged homicides he has perpetrated on the West Coast and possibly San Francisco." The letter includes a San Francisco Police Department Information Bulletin dated July 12, 1974, concerning a list of "gay-related unsolved murders which have occurred in this city."

The bulletin offers three semi-detailed incidents where suspected gay males were stabbed to death via multiple wounds. The second page of the bulletin lists thirty-five unsolved murders in the jurisdiction, most during the time period when Zamastil was thought to be in the area. Causes of death range from stabbing to beating, and from strangulation to bludgeoning. It should be noted that Zamastil has mentioned his propensity for gay-related sex if the need arises. He also used multiple weapons in his murders.

In October 1979, a detective from the Mohave County (Arizona) Sheriff's Department near Las Vegas contacted the Sauk County Sheriff's Department in Wisconsin to inquire about and offer synopses of six unsolved cases that could be linked to Zamastil. It appears Zamastil was in the area during the times of these murders.

Victim #1
- white female
- from Needles, California
- strangled with her bra
- nude

Victim #2
- white male
- shot two times
- buried in a shallow grave

Victim #3
- white female
- cause of death was either stabbing or shooting

Victim #4
- white male
- one gunshot wound

Victim #5
- white male
- massive blows to the head

Victim #6
- white male
- gunshot wound

Two cases, in particular, raised the interest of detectives. On September 9, 1975, the body of Deborah Carrick was found near Grand Canyon National Park in Arizona. She had suffered blunt force trauma to the head. Even before her body was located, her personal ID was located near Santa Rosa, California, a vicinity with a morbid history as a body dump site.

A cold case team worked hard to match Zamastil to this young woman's murder. Multiple serial killers were "working" in the area at the time, flooding the landscape with death. In fact, four other women's bodies were located in the vicinity, offering investigators the idea that there was at least one other killer "plying his trade." Still, Zamastil seemed to fit the bill. He worked as a tow truck driver in the Mojave Desert area. He was out of prison and in the area. One of the cold case detectives offered that "in one of Zamastil's murders, he ordered the victim to dress after raping her." Carrick was fully clothed except for shoes and socks.

In a parallel story, there was another murder in the area, that of a young man, on August 18, 1975. Two men were arrested and convicted of that killing. They later admitted to killing Ms. Carrick, then recanted.

A case with even more promise of ties to Zamastil was the September 5, 1977, murder of twenty-one-year-old Scott Allison, a military man who was traveling home to see his family. Allison pulled off the main road less than 100 miles from home to grab a quick nap near the malevolent desert abutting San Bernardino before heading out on the final leg of his journey. However, he never woke up. Allison's head was bashed in with a rock and his 1977 Chevy Monza was missing.

The Mojave Desert can be a foreboding place of its own accord, but used as a body dump site, it becomes a scene from a horror movie. Joe Nelson, a reporter for a collection of newspapers, penned an article on November 13, 2013, entitled "High Desert Known for Body Dumping." In the article, he offers "the skeletal remains of four people, unearthed from two shallow graves on Wednesday ... left some pondering the darker side of the Mojave." In that same story, a former San Bernardino deputy sheriff opines, "If there were to be a cross everywhere someone dumped a body, the desert would look like Forest Lawn."

Another body dump site, near an area known as Menchala Flats in the California desert, resembles an apocalyptic landscape with only a deserted, one-room shack barely standing. In the surrounding area, protruding from the ground, is a strange, lonely object that looks like the withered remains of a sweat lodge. There is an abandoned truck cab, a bed frame, and a burnt out, ash-laden fire pit. All of these inanimate, washed out, desiccated objects stand watch over the abandoned bodies of those once living.

While the above cases linked to Zamastil are cold and unsolved, there is undisputed human carnage in his wake. In a taped interview with Chief Deputy Gorski of the Sauk County (Wisconsin) Sheriff's Department on August 18, 1978, Zamastil admits to two murders of unnamed persons in the west. One incident occurred in Hollywood, California, around June 5, 1977, following an altercation with a "Hispanic-looking male." Zamastil says he stabbed the man five or six times, causing his death. Zamastil also told Borski that he choked a man "a little bit" in Long Beach, California, in December, most likely that same year.

Zamastil later picked up a girl in Los Angeles. He described her as five-feet-eight, white with a slim build, and approximately thirty-three years old. Her name was Sandy. Zamastil stated the two of them stayed a night in a motel, registering in his name. The next day they drove down the coastal highway to somewhere near La Jolla, California. During this stop, Zamastil states he "pushed the girl down a rocky mountainside and left her." He then "threw her bag alongside the road." He believed the girl to be dead.

The following information relates to the cases of three known victims for which Zamastil has been sentenced to life in prison.

Leesa Jo Shaner
May 29, 1973

Leesa was a young and pretty mother, wife, and daughter who resided in the Tucson, Arizona, area. On the above date at around 9:30 p.m., she drove to Tucson International Airport to pick up her husband, Gary. He had been discharged from the military and was returning home from Japan.

Leesa was excited and eager to reunite with her husband. Maybe too excited. Jim Miller, Leesa's father and an FBI agent, implored his daughter to allow him to accompany her on the trip. Leesa declined and off she went, likely giddy with expectation.

About 10:30 that night, Gary called Leesa's family to ascertain who was picking him up at the airport. Alarmed that Leesa had not arrived at the airport, Agent Miller sent family members to check out alternate routes she could have taken. Miller himself went directly to the airport, searching every locale there and questioning staff persons. In what is probably a parent's most gut-wrenching nightmare, he did find his daughter's car. It was empty, with the driver's side window partially down. Her purse was open on the front seat. The keys and parking stub were gone. Leesa had vanished.

A massive law enforcement investigation ensued and agencies rallied to their police brother-in-arms in his quest to find his missing, likely abducted daughter. (Note: many officials use the term kidnapped when the expected outcome is a ransom demand. Abduction is often used when the crime takes on a more nefarious motive: usually sexual assault and murder.)

It is common knowledge that no police agency would allow any relative of a crime victim, much less a father, to take an active role in an investigation. Emotions can trump good investigative work. The highs and lows of an investigation can wreak havoc on the victim's family even without professional family investment. Being so close to an active investigation can be hellacious. Consequently, three FBI agents were assigned to the case. Since this was a presumed kidnapping investigation, the FBI took the lead. This decision would dramatically change in the months ahead.

The leads were scarce despite countless hours invested into the investigation. In fact, to those not in the know, progress likely seemed minimal at best. That changed about four months after her disappearance, when on May 23, 1973, three men searching for Native American relics and curios on the Fort Huachuca Reservation in Arizona stumbled upon a skull. The following day, US Army Criminal Investigative agents located Leesa's nude and badly decomposed skeletal remains.

The crime fell under federal jurisdiction since this property is a United States Army training facility, hence the involvement of the FBI. Leesa could only be identified by her wedding ring, which oddly, her killer did not steal. There had been much rain and there was little evidence left at the scene.

The massive investigation continued into determining who killed Leesa, but seemed to slow with each passing year. One newspaper article offered that agents had accumulated the names of 7,701 individuals in the course of the search. One agent stated: "Here's our list of suspects," and dropped a huge stack of papers, files and notes on a desk. The list included names of 7,701 men assigned to the fort where Leesa's remains were found. Leesa's father had offered a $10,000 reward for any useful information.

Suspects were myriad, including a suspected serial killer in Gregory Barker. Barker, thought to have committed sixteen murders, was involved in the sexual assault and murder of Hilda Roche in Alexandria, Virginia, in 1982. In April of that year, a body later identified as Ms. Roche, was located in a rural, wooded area. She had been bound and raped in the bedroom of her apartment, shot execution-style in the back of the head, and left brazenly lying on her back, nude except for a pair of shoes. DNA and fingerprints led investigators to focus on Barker.

Barker was an interesting character. He served two tours in Vietnam, rising to the rank of captain, and was awarded a Purple Heart. But upon returning to civilian life, this very bright man's life took a strange turn to the dark side. He became a bank robber and took on aliases. He would spend countless nights wandering the streets, then sleeping in all-night movie theatres. One alias he used was Alexander Graham, which was a somewhat humorous choice for a person working in the phone room as a telemarketer for a radio station. It was here he was arrested the day after a nationally syndicated television show featured him.

On April 24, 1991, with the help of the TV show *America's Most Wanted*, Barker was located and arrested for bank robbery, as well as the murder of Hilda Roche and the possible murder of Leesa Jo Shaner. Agents were ecstatic to have Barker in custody and requested an interview regarding the murder of Leesa. The request was denied by law enforcement, and agents were stymied in moving the investigation forward. Later, the agents did have a brief opportunity to meet with Barker due to the fact that he acknowledged he was at Fort Huachuca when Leesa was murdered. He indicated he had heard of the case.

This piqued the agents' interest, so a polygraph test followed. Barker showed "some signs of deceit." This could simply have been a nervousness due to him possibly being a serial killer. But there would be no further instances of "cooperation," and Barker denied any further knowledge of the murder.

Enter William Zamastil, who was in custody in Wisconsin. Zamastil sent a letter to an FBI special agent in Milwaukee on May 20, 1981, wishing to discuss the murder of "a female by the name of Leesa Jo in Tucson, Arizona." He also wanted to discuss the killing of a female outside of Las Vegas, Nevada, "who was found in a mine shaft."

Like many incarcerated serial killers, Zamastil was full of bombast, braggadocio, and bluster, regaling his cellmate with tales from the crypt about his killings. It seems these killing machines cannot keep their egregious acts to themselves. Zamastil told his cellmate that he had killed a "cop's kid," who was a federal agent's son, out west, and had buried the body on a military base. In later interviews, Zamastil went on to say Leesa begged him for her life, and stated her dad was an FBI agent. Agent Luell suggests "this even excited the killer more." Recall that Zamastil had once been stationed at Fort Huachuca, where Leesa's body had been found.

When Agent Luell returned from retirement as part of a Department of Justice cold case grant, numerous unsolved cases were included in the $500,000 grant mandate. Luell learned of Zamastil's version of the murdered "cop's son" out west during the course of these case investigations and his meeting with the jailhouse informant. Luell then contacted the FBI, and the rest is history.

Zamastil was charged with and convicted in 2009 of the first degree intentional murder of Leesa Jo Shaner. He was flown to Arizona from Wisconsin for the trial on a chartered flight, guarded by United States Marshals. Zamastil received a life sentence for Leesa's killing and is serving this sentence concurrently with his Wisconsin case. Part of the agreement allowed Zamastil to serve his sentences in Wisconsin. Zamastil denies killing Leesa and has appealed the conviction. Leesa's father, FBI Agent Jim Miller, had passed away two years earlier. A week after the indictment came down for Leesa's murder, Zamastil was considered a person of interest in the murder of Christine Rothschild in Madison.

Interestingly, one individual who testified against Zamastil was Lawrence Dalton, another serial killer with Wisconsin ties. On April 22, 1979, law enforcement officials announced that a woman's body had been unearthed in front of a home in Kenosha, Wisconsin. Dalton had previously resided at the address. Twenty-five-year-old Blanchie Penna, from nearby Racine, had been missing since 1977.

Dalton was also sought in the sexual assault and murder of a twelve-year-old girl less than twenty miles away in Waukegan, Illinois, and was a suspect in two murders in Cleveland, Ohio, along with the killing of a "Jane Doe" victim in Lake County, Illinois. He was convicted of three murders and a sexual assault on November 18, 1981.

Authorities list his "body count" at four and counting. Dalton has numerous suicide attempts in prison. He attempted to hang himself in one instance, and in another starvation necessitated force feeding.

Jacqueline and Malcolm Bradshaw
February, 1978

According to extremely detailed police accounts from multiple jurisdictions, a pair of siblings, Malcolm (17), and Jacqueline (18) Bradshaw, left their home in Canoga Park, California, on February 25, 1978, in the company of Ron Pucillo, Jackie's boyfriend. They headed to Las Vegas on an errand. Arriving in Las Vegas early the next day, the trio rented a motel room and slept until early evening. Pucillo's truck hit a pothole while cruising around Las Vegas, forcing the group to hitch a ride back to their motel.

On February 27, 1978, the Bradshaw siblings left Pucillo and were intent on hitchhiking back to their home. They were next seen at a gas station in Barstow, California, sometime in the late afternoon. They were in the company of a "white male adult with sandy-colored hair, driving a small pickup with two suitcases in the bed." Jackie called her mother, Caroline, to let her know they were coming back home and were getting a ride from a "nice guy." The Bradshaw children never returned home nor seen alive again. Their mother began a personal crusade to find her children.

Caroline reported her kids missing to the Los Angeles Police Department on February 28, 1978. She then traveled to the Barstow area to canvas all the gas stations, eventually finding the one where the siblings were last seen. She brought photos of the kids to ascertain if someone could identify them, and eventually an employee at a GoLo Station recognized them, offering that they were in the company of another man with a pickup truck. Caroline supplied all this information to the Los Angeles police, and on March 10, 1978, detectives traveled to Barstow to obtain statements from GoLo staff and customers.

One of the investigators prepared an Identi-Kit composite of the man last seen with the Bradshaws. The police report interjects the following: "When a booking photograph of William Zamastil from that time period is compared to the "Identi-Kit composite, one sees several similarities between the two photographs."

On March 26, 1978, a local sheep herder stumbled upon the naked bodies of the Bradshaws, who had been murdered in the desert thirteen miles south of Barstow. Malcolm was semi-nude and lying in a face-down position. It appeared his body was elevated over some debris to facilitate a sexual assault. Jacqueline was completely nude save for one item of clothing. The ground near the bodies appeared disturbed, as if there had been a struggle. Pieces of jewelry seemed to have been ripped off during that struggle.

Based on the crime scene evidence as well as professional experience, an investigator in the case offered the following investigative opinion:

• The pair were killed by one male assailant who gained their confidence by offering the victims a ride to Los Angeles.

- The sexual assaults and murders occurred on February 27, 1978, after leaving the point they were picked up by the assailant.
- The two were murdered by blunt force trauma to their heads with the same or similar-sized weapon.
- The pair were victims of robbery because their belongings (suitcases, jewelry, and items) were stolen from them.

Authorities notified Caroline Bradshaw that the bodies of her children were located in a desolate strip of arid land. She traveled to the area to identify pieces of jewelry located at the scene, as well as on the body of Jacqueline. The jewelry was identified as among her daughter's possessions. However, two suitcases, one bearing the name "Craig" and the other an orange-striped yellow suitcase, were both missing, presumed stolen by the killer.

Autopsies were performed on the Bradshaw siblings on March 28, 1978. Both sustained blunt force injuries to the head, which was the ultimate cause of death. Jacqueline had suffered "apparent strangulation," as some clothing was tied around her neck. Sexual assault of both victims was suspected.

The Bradshaw case remained unsolved until Zamastil was arrested for the sexual assault and murder of Mary Johnson in southern Wisconsin on August 1, 1978. It was at this time that the pieces of the Bradshaw puzzle began to fall into place. When Zamastil was arrested, there was a suitcase in his possession that was light brown in color with yellow stripes. Also located were a set of keys, along with a silver and turquoise ring. Later on, the suitcase and ring were identified by Caroline Bradshaw as belonging to her children.

Gazing Into the Abyss

On August 13, 1978, a San Bernardino County (California) homicide detective contacted the Sauk County Sheriff's Office regarding the suitcase found in Zamastil's possession at the time of his arrest. One day later, that same detective spoke with Zamastil over the phone in tape-recorded conversations concerning some unsolved murders in the California jurisdiction. It was during this conversation that Zamastil admitted to "committing a double murder of a teenage male and female in Barstow in 1978, and one of them had a big hole in his head."

August 18, 1984, was a day of reckoning for Zamastil. He sent a letter to an assistant district attorney in San Bernardino, agreeing to extradition and a guilty plea in the Bradshaw case in return for a concurrent sentence to his life term on the Mary Johnson case in Wisconsin. A criminal complaint was filed on June 18, 2003, charging Zamastil with two counts of murder and two counts of robbery in conjunction with the killings of the Bradshaws.

September 2003 was the "Waterloo" for Zamastil. He signed a waiver of extradition and was transported back to California to face the charges against him. Zamastil denies these killings and has verbalized his intention to appeal.

"Murder is a talent we all possess."

- ***Unknown***

Chapter 8

Is There Such a Thing as a Serial Killer Wannabe?

Surely William Zamastil, by virtue of the number of his known and suspected murder victims, is a serial killer. There is no debating that fact. He fits the standard profile to a tee simply due to the sheer number of his victims. But what of the individuals who "strive" to reach the pinnacle of murderous fame, only to fall short of the obligatory number of victims? Where are they on the continuum of serial offending?

Historically, the serial killer has been judged, rated, and categorized by the number of kills – the amount of dead and totality of carnage. This is a totally quantitative method of measuring an offender, limiting debate of who is and who is not a serial killer. James Fox and Jack Levin, in their book *Extreme Killing*, offer the following thoughts on the serial killer "wannabe" concept:

"There has even been disagreement about the minimum victim tally to establish a repetition of killing as serial. Some defined serial murder as at least four murders separated in time, whereas others preferred a body count of three."

Fox and Levin go on to offer that lowering the minimum victim count to include offenders who have the potential for serial status should not be considered, even if their murdering career is derailed by circumstances such as incarceration.

Criminologist Eric Hickey counters with, "Many want-to-be serial killers end up in prison after their first murder." He adds, "The essence of individuals who desire to be serial killers is more important than the act of killing itself."

In the relatively recent past, a smattering of scholars, practitioners, and criminologists have begun looking into the idea of a qualitative method or description of killers with sexual proclivities, referring to this phenomenon as possibly a Serial Killer Syndrome. This idea would expand the concept by which killers, although stymied in their "careers," exude the potential to take many lives if not for intervening forces.

What are potential roadblocks in a killer's path to becoming the pinnacle predator?

Advances in the use of DNA as an investigative tool enhance the possibility that a killer can be apprehended after committing one murder instead of waiting until he commits more murders.

Arrest and incarceration are certainly intervening factors. If a person enters the criminal justice system after one murder or sexual assault, that system has cut the quantity of victims, but the Serial Killer Syndrome remains with the individual.

Similar to prison incarceration is the institutionalization in some type of mental health facility, long-term treatment program, or locked forensic hospital. All of these forced placements would remove a killer from the community prior to more victims falling prey.

How would an interrupted serial killer differ from a full blown episodic murderer?

Possibly only in number of kills. There are several stages in the development of a serial killer.

Development of a Serial Killer

We know from research that many serial killers can emanate from a basic background boilerplate. As previously mentioned, Dr. Helen Morrison calls serial killers "cookie cutter killers" as their histories are so similar. These perpetrators were abused in some form, either physically, emotionally, or sexually. Much of the abuse typically involves severe, torturous, and near-death violence, featuring weapons such as pipes, boards, or hammer hits to the head. Emotional abuse might have included verbal degrading, name calling, or even dressing a male child as a girl and curling his hair during his years in elementary school.

Sexual abuse knows no bounds in these horrific family situations. These cases can include forcing children to have sex with strange adults, scalding of sex organs, or worse. These budding offenders typically have poor coping skills, engage in petty, pre-killing behaviors, and often regress deeply into a vivid fantasy world of savage, brutal, bizarre, and perverted sexual activity. The fantasy becomes so engrained and omnipresent in their lives that it is often difficult for the offender to think of anything else.

Westley Dodd was a mysoped, which is a pedophile who abducts children for sexual purposes and then murders them. Dodd indicated he could think of nothing else but sexually assaulting and murdering children. While sleeping with one young victim, Dodd would lean over and whisper, "I'm going to kill you in the morning." He also kept his victims confined in a closet encased in a homemade trap while he was at work. Dodd was convicted of the 1989 murders of three children and the attempted kidnapping of another child, and executed by the state of Washington in 1993.

Involvement in sexual activity precludes any type of intimacy. Rather, it offers the offender a chance at dominance and control over an individual, whether they be they male, female, or child.

Many offenders harbor numerous paraphilias, fueling

their ever-growing fantasy. A paraphilia is defined as "a condition in which a person's sexual arousal and gratification depends on fantasizing and/or engaging in sexual behavior that is atypical or unusual." A few paraphilias furnished by criminologist and educator Dallas Drake, from the Center for Homicide Research in Minneapolis, include: haematophilia (love of blood); urophilia (attraction to urine); zoophilia (sex with animals); and necrophilia (sex with the dead).

One Ohio multiple killer, Matthew Hoffman, engaged in dendrophilia, which is sexual arousal by trees or leaves. Hoffman murdered three members of a stranger's family, dismembered them, and hid their bodies in hollowed-out trees. He kidnapped a teenager from the same family, keeping her chained in a room on a stockpiled bed of leaves. The home appeared to be insulated by bags of leaves.

Then there are the infamous attack paraphilias:

Picquerism is repetitive stabbing, with a numbers count of twelve or more wounds and the stabbing being sexual in nature. Drake believes slasher attacks often combine stabbing and cutting with the victim's screams and shrieks for maximum gratification for the attacker. The noted serial killer researcher offers, "This paraphilia expresses sexuality by penetrating the victim with a knife. The victim's screams, the bloodletting, the odors all creates sexual experience for the killer."

Blastophilia involves the frenzied actions of ripping and tearing of clothing, or snipping fabric with scissors. Included in this can be a struggle and the look of fright on the victim. Drake offers that "sadism is a salient factor in attacks."

Other attack or dangerous paraphilias are:
- Erotophonilia – love of murder
- Infibulations – genital mutilation
- Asphyxiophilia – strangulation or suffocation
- Symphorophilia – staging a disaster

There are numerous other paraphilias. For example, the 1996 movie *Crash* depicted a couple who became sexually aroused by car crashes and sought out the subculture of those injured to reignite their sex life.

The Macdonald Triad

Present in many serial killers is a phenomenon known as the Macdonald Triad (also referred to as the triad of homicide or triad of sociopathy), developed in 1963 by John Macdonald, who was engaged in studying a number of both psychotic and non-psychotic patients. His findings suggested that a grouping of three behaviors were often present in "very sadistic patients." These were bed wetting past a certain age, fire setting, and cruelty, especially the torture and abuse of animals. These animals are usually smaller creatures, but some are as large as horses. Many offenders, both serial and non-serial, have histories of such behaviors.

Certainly there is more to a serial killer than the above behaviors and beliefs. The point is that there are offenders with the same or similar backgrounds who only kill or attempt to kill one victim. The wannabe serial killer with only one victim should be considered on the spectrum of serial offenders.

A Definition of Serial Killer

Stephen Giannangelo, in his detailed book: *Real-Life Monsters: A Psychological Examination of the Serial Murderer*, offers a concise definition of the interrupted serial killer or wannabe. He writes:

"A Serial Killer: Repetitive, cyclical activity usually associated with a buildup of tension, committing the crime, and a cooling off period. Actual numbers are unimportant; what is relevant is the compulsion to repetitively commit the crime and the murder is a psychological necessity, not incidental to other crime." He goes on to state, "Predatory murderers are individuals who commit crimes for personal enjoyment, including sexual pleasure."

Giannangelo agrees that the number of murders is secondary to mindset, behavioral proclivities, and the ultimate addiction to murder.

All of the following killers are predatory in nature:

Lawrence Singleton

Singleton could well be the epitome of an interrupted serial killer due to the voraciousness of his sexual desires.

On September 29, 1978, this offender stopped to pick up a hitchhiking fifteen-year-old Mary Vincent in California. However, being a Good Samaritan was nowhere in Singleton's plans. He took Mary to a secluded spot where he repeatedly raped her. Then, either to complete his wanton desires or hide the evidence of his crime, he took a hatchet, severed both of Mary's arms at the elbows, and threw her off a forty-foot cliff, where she landed naked, mutilated, and near death.

Mary, with what must have been a burning will to live, pulled herself back to the crime scene. She flagged down a passerby who actually was a Good Samaritan, and he drove Mary to a local hospital. She had prosthetic arms by the time Singleton was arrested.

Six months after the arrest, Singleton was sentenced to fourteen years in prison for rape, kidnapping, mayhem, attempted murder, and sex crimes. He served only eight years of the sentence and after his release was not welcome in any community. He was forced to live on the grounds of San Quentin Prison until his parole discharged.

Writer Amanda Spake, who interviewed Singleton while he was in San Quentin, had this to say about Singleton's case on a murder-related website: "What was most surprising to me, however, was not his sentence. It was that Larry Singleton had worked his crimes around in his mind so completely that they did not warrant punishment at all."

Singleton relocated to his former home state of Florida when free of the constraints of California law. He was convicted of petty theft on two occasions in 1990, but this was the least of his criminality. A neighbor phoned police early in 1997 to report what sounded like Singleton assaulting a woman in his apartment. When police arrived, they were greeted at the door by Singleton with knife in hand and covered in blood. On the floor was the body of Roxanne Hayes. She had been stabbed multiple times in what appeared to be a murderous frenzy.

John Weber

When John Weber finally went to trial for crimes committed in rural northern Wisconsin in the spring of 1989, it was said that he looked like a crazed werewolf not yet returned to human form. For example, the fur mask he wore was reportedly because his defense team wanted him to look as though he was not in control of his faculties, thereby aiding in a not guilty by reason of insanity or mental defect judgement. It was not difficult for the citizenry of Price County, Wisconsin, to envision Weber as a monster, as less than human, when his crimes came to light.

A city of Phillips teenager, Carla Lenz, left home for a "few minutes" on November 11, 1986. She was never seen again until her mostly decomposed body was dug up a number of years later. What had been done to her was incomprehensible.

Two years later, Weber contacted the Phillips Police Department to report his wife, Emily (Carla Lenz's older sister), had been abducted, raped, beaten by three men, and left naked in the woods. After miraculously escaping her tormentors, Weber told police that Emily made her way home, where relatives transported her to a hospital.

Eventually, it was learned that Weber had taken his wife to a secluded corner of the family property and proceeded to beat her mercilessly. He cut off her clothing, burned her with lit cigars, and stabbed her in numerous parts of her body. She was sodomized with foreign objects, then beaten in the head with a shovel. During this onslaught of brutality, Weber uttered something to the effect of, "I am going to kill you like I did Carla."

Obviously, Weber now was the prime suspect in the disappearance of his sister-in-law. Police expanded their investigation to include the first victim and learned what was done to her. Although similar to the attacks on Emily, these were even more hideous.

Police located an audio tape during a search of Weber's truck that featured Weber's voice detailing each and every gut-wrenching perversion heaped upon Carla, culminating in the statement that he had cut off slices of her flesh and consumed it.

Weber's sexual fantasies included bondage, rape, cannibalism and more. He stated he had to leave his workstation multiple times per day to masturbate in an effort to satiate his fantasy. Weber denied that the activities on the tape happened; however, the ghastly retelling of a young woman's death throes was convincing to the jury.

Joe Clark

Joe Clark exhibited extremely interesting behaviors as a young man. At the age of seventeen, he enjoyed stalking, capturing, and holding other youngsters against their will in his closet. What happened later was even more sinister.

In 1994, the parents of fourteen-year-old Christopher Steiner informed authorities that their son went missing from home. Police found a cut screen and muddy footprints in various rooms of their house. Chris was found a week later, his body lying over a fallen tree on a sandbar. Strangely, no obvious injuries were noted at the autopsy, but investigators were certain this was a murder.

The same event seemingly happened again on July, 29, 1995. Thad Phillips, another area youth, woke up and found himself being carried, dragged, hoisted, and ordered to run. Still in the partial throes of sleep, Thad complied. He would come to regret this decision.

Clark took his victim to an old, filthy hovel-like house and proceeded to grab, twist, pull, and manipulate Thad's ankle bone until it snapped. Clark then went for the leg, breaking this extremity. Adding to what was seemingly a violent, bizarre, sexual fantasy, the perpetrator then bound Thad's wounds in makeshift, sock-like casts. Thad attempted to get away on multiple instances, eventually dragging himself to a phone and dialing 911 as his nightmare was just beginning to end.

Thad had multiple surgeries as a result of his injuries and Clark was sentenced to 100 years in prison, but the nightmare wasn't over after all. Law enforcement noticed similarities in the assaults of Thad Phillips and Chris Steiner, and exhumed Chris's body for further investigation. Clark pleaded not guilty to the Steiner murder, but was found guilty by a jury.

Clark had exhibited numerous abhorrent sexual behaviors. He stalked victims and entered homes when people were in residence. He enjoyed, and most likely felt a sexual rush from breaking bones and hearing the snapping noise that accompanied the actions. Lastly, he had a fetish for white athletic socks, specifically smelling them.

William Marquardt

A burglar with a history of killing animals, William Marquardt was arrested in 2006 and charged with murdering his mother, Mary Jane Marquardt, in Chippewa County, Wisconsin. He was found not guilty by reason of mental defect and placed in the state's maximum security ward located in Mendota. The placement was for seventy-five years for animal cruelty, including the killing of three dogs and three pet rabbits.

Soon after the murder of his mother, Marquardt was brought to Florida to stand trial for the 2000 stabbing and shooting of Margaret Ruiz and her daughter, Esperanza Wells. Marquardt was known to have been in Florida at the time. Blood from the two women was found on the knife in Marquardt had in his possession upon arrest in Wisconsin. In his defense, Marquardt attempted to promote the idea that he was set up by drug dealers. This defense failed and he was sentenced to death in Florida.

The Chippewa County district attorney offered the following summary of the Wisconsin and Florida cases: "The investigations fit together like a jigsaw puzzle. Once complete, the puzzle will portray the image of a serial killer."

Steven Zelich

Another case of interest is that of disgraced West Allis, Wisconsin, police officer Steven Zelich. The former cop originally was arrested for secreting the dismembered corpses of two women in suitcases, allegedly after killing them. The suitcases were found on the side of the road in Walworth County, Wisconsin.

Zelich was an aficionado of bondage/sadism/masochism and a habitué of websites, chat rooms, and Craigslist. He used the tag "Mr. Handcuffs." He frequented these dark sites trolling for like-minded women. According to CBS 58 News in Milwaukee, a portion of his profile read: "There's nothing better than a slave tied tight, gagged, blindfolded, hooded, chained ..."

Zelich has two known victims. The first was Laura Simonson of Minnesota, who was found naked with a rope around her neck. The second victim, unnamed, was found with her hands bound and covered in garbage bags. It is believed Zelich also attempted to kill a woman in 2001, but failed.

Brandon Wilson

Brandon Wilson, a compulsive drifter from western Wisconsin, was on probation for numerous offenses including auto theft and desecration of a graveyard. He was deep into the world of illicit drugs. On November 14, 1998, this young offender, who had homicidal ideas about killing his mother and engaging in sex with the dead, brought his deviant fantasies to life.

While squatting at a campground near Oceanside, California, his desire to kill became overwhelming. He selected a "hunting ground," and his monstrous game was afoot.

Wilson passed on the opportunity to kill two women he chanced upon while searching for a suitable victim before homing in on his perfect prey. He followed a nine-year-old boy into a park lavatory and stabbed him to death. He was caught a few days later when he attacked a woman in Los Angeles.

Wilson gleefully admitted he would have kept killing had he not been caught. When in custody, this burgeoning killer re-enacted the murder of the boy, smiling while pretending to stab the detective, who was playing the victim.

Additional Arguments

Enzo Yaksic, serial killer expert and founder of the Serial Homicide Expertise and Information Sharing Collaborative, takes the idea of adding offenders with fewer victims to the category of serial murder one step further. In his scholarly paper *The Folly of Counting Bodies*, Yaksic offers that individuals who may or may not have killed anyone, but engaged in extremely violent verbiage, activities or fantasies, could be considered "would-bes." Yaksic also uses the terms "potential killer, fledgling or budding" individuals.

Yaksic quotes a collection of authors led by Matt DeLisi, professor of sociology at Iowa State University, regarding the concept of homicidal ideation: the process of thinking about, plotting, or planning murder. Yaksic culled together a list of forty persons (thirty since 2010) who he believes fit his theory. Among the forty listed are the following:

• Daniel Stani-Reginald, who completed 9,000 internet searches on serial killers

• Ben Moynihan compared himself to serial killers.

• James Caldwell wanted to harm strangers.

• Mario Swain was a serial killer in training. He kept notebooks and license plate numbers on women he wanted to kill. (1 victim)

• Terique Hall had the markings of somebody who was very disturbed (1 victim).

• Nathaniel Sebastian was a super-fan of John Gacy.

Yaksic's paper offers statements from various criminal justice professionals regarding the concept of wannabe, would-be, or could-be serial killers with only one kill. For instance, a Honolulu man named Randall Saito shot and stabbed Sandra Yamashiro in 1979. He had only one victim, but was mentioned as fitting "all the criteria of a classic serial killer" by the prosecutor in his case. He was diagnosed with sexual sadism and necrophilia. The prosecutor also suggested that because Saito committed a murder, "he had the inherent ability to commit another murder."

In a second example of Yaksic's theory, Sgt. David Walker of the Tulsa, Oklahoma, Police Department's Homicide Division, said of serial shooter Brennon Lovett: "It was an interesting study in killing due to the high number of shooting attempts attributed to him." Lovett was responsible for six random shootings in the area. One victim, Wayne Bell, died from gunshot wounds. Sgt. Walker went on the suggest Lovett's mindset was that of a "serial killer who was only successful once."

Discussion Questions

1) Do you think there is such a thing as a serial killer "wannabe" or a serial killer "could be" if not for interruption by the system?

2) Do you think serial killers should only be labeled by number of victims, or is there a "Serial Killer Syndrome"?

3) Do you think there is a method to legally track behaviors/warning signs before someone kills their first victim? If so, should this type of person be institutionalized for preventive detention purposes?

4) Do the killers in the above case examples show signs of aspiring to be serial killers?

5) Can a person be considered a "wannabe" even if they have never killed anyone?

Chapter 9

Do We Need a New Category of Multiple Murder?

A Suggestion for Typing Homicide

The following unpublished article emanated from a number of discussions among students of homicide. As mentioned earlier, criminologists, researchers, and criminal justice professionals have had a difficult time arriving at a consensus on the terminology and definition of multiple homicide. I feel this article is relevant to this book as well as to the ongoing discussions of multiple murder. Hopefully, it will serve as both a prologue as well as an epilogue.

Introduction

A rapid succession of very high-profile crimes spread throughout the nation in the late 1940s through the early 1960s. These crimes grabbed the attention of the media, stoked fear in the citizenry, and challenged the criminal justice system.

- William Heirens, who came to be labeled the Lipstick Killer by the Chicago media because of the messages left written on his victim's mirror: "Catch me, I can't stop killing." Heirens confessed to killing three persons over a period of seven months in 1946.
- Howard Unruh calmly walked through his Camden, New Jersey, neighborhood murdering thirteen people, including three children, in a twelve-minute fusillade of bullets on September 6, 1949.
- Charles Starkweather traversed Nebraska and Wyoming, murdering eleven people from December 1957 through January 1958.
- Harvey Glatman, a self-styled photographer, was dubbed the Lonely Hearts Killer. He would place ads in Los Angeles-area newspapers looking for "models." A number of women answered these requests and were later found bound and murdered in the deserts around southern California in 1957.
- Ex-convicts Perry Smith and Richard Hickock invaded a Nebraska farmhouse in November 1959, murdering the entire Clutter family of four for a radio and a few dollars.
- Over a span of three years from 1962-1964, someone was entering women's apartments in Boston, raping and strangling them in a very similar fashion. The victim count was thirteen, and the perpetrator was dubbed the

Boston Strangler. Albert DeSalvo later admitted to the killings and was committed to a state psychiatric facility.

- An unemployed drifter named Richard Speck broke into a Chicago nursing school residence in August 1966, binding and subsequently stabbing to death eight student nurses. (There were nine nurses, but one hid under the bed and the offender apparently lost count.)
- Charles Whitman scaled the University of Texas bell tower and opened fire on the crowd below in September 1966, slaying sixteen people and wounding thirty-two more.

Although these examples were very diverse crimes with different victim counts, methods of criminal operation, and offender typologies, the media and authorities labeled them all as mass murders or multiple killings, with none of the delineation we know today. In fact, "as recently as 1982, there was only one term used to describe murderers who killed many victims: mass murderers." *(Keppel, 1997)*

However, over the years, criminologists, researchers, and law enforcement began to notice that this singular term did not adequately define or describe the various types of murder.

A New Way to Type Homicide

In the modern study of violent crime, most criminologists agree that there are six types of murder, five of which are listed generally as various types of multicide. Multicide is a crime of murder committed by one offender with more than one victim.

Murder Typologies
(Douglas, 1992)

Type	# of Victims	Victim Location
Single	1	On site
Double	2	Same location
Triple	3	Same location
Mass	4 or more	Same location
Bifurcated Mass *(new concept - see note below*	4 or more	Separate locations
Spree	2 or more	Separate locations
Serial	2 or more	Separate locations

The first typology is a single homicide. Simply put, it is a one-victim murder. After this, the remaining typologies suggest multiple victims ranging from two victims to scores of killed attributed to the perpetrator(s), and with victims in various locations.

Single Location / Multiple Murders

A double homicide is two victims in one location as a result of one criminal event. An offender robs a gas station and kills the clerk and another customer. This is followed by a triple homicide in which there are three victims at the scene. This also results from a single event.

Mass Murder

Mass murder is four or more victims in one location, occurring in one act. Mass murder can be committed for any number of reasons. For example, many school shooters, workplace killers, and family annihilators are considered mass murderers.

Historically, mass murderers were found on scene, dead by their own hand, often by a single gunshot wound to the head. Later, this same type of criminal baited police into shooting him/her in what then became known as suicide by cop. In recent forensic history, a select number of family mass murderers actually flee the scene and become fugitives. (John List, Christian Longo, and Ramon Salcido are examples of family killers eschewing suicide in favor of an attempt of life on the run.)

Felony Mass Murder

The deaths of four or more victims in the course of another crime is called a felony-related mass murder. *(Duwe, 2007)* The 2000 murder of four individuals in an ATM theft by the Carr brothers in Wichita, Kansas, is an example of this type of crime.

The Carrs broke into an apartment, forced the victims to engage in sexual acts, then herded the victims into a vehicle and drove to the ATM. After draining the money machine, the victims were forced to kneel in the winter cold, wearing only their underwear, and were then shot execution-style in the head.

This type of crime also includes multi-victim home invasions where offenders force themselves into the home of an unsuspecting family for the purpose of robbery, then kill the entire group of residents.

Note 1: Criminologists have begun discussing a new concept in this type of crime, calling it the bifurcated mass murder. This addition to the mass murder discussion focuses on the idea that a significant number of mass murders take place in two locations. Either the crimes begin at the perpetrator's home and then move to a public locale, or the rampage begins in a public forum and moves to another public area. *(Hickey, 2014, lecture notes)*

Multiple Location / Multiple Murders
Spree Killings

One category of killer that engages in a multi-location, multi-victim rampage is called a spree killer. *(Douglas, et al., 1992)* This is a crime with two or more victims in separate locations as the result of a continuing event.

This type of multiple murder often involves carjacking, robberies, abductions, possibly sexual assault, and myriad other crimes. This is one event, with no cooling-off period between crimes. The offender(s) is fully aware of the police presence amassed and is often considered a fugitive. The police chase is part of the continuing excitation.

The offender's vehicle not only serves as a means of evading police, it also serves as an arsenal as well as a house on wheels. It is often full of dirty clothes, fast food wrappers, maps, and newspapers following the crime. Blaring music and the consumption of drugs often adds to the excitement of the chase. If the offender does not take his own life on scene just prior to arrest, the individual may claim exhaustion. Officers state that fugitives can sometimes have a musk-like odor. This could very well be from poor hygiene or the stench of excitement.

Spree murder is like serial murder at warp speed, or as some describe it, a mobile mass murder or a lethal binge.

Case Study

An example of a spree killer is the case of Christopher Dorner, the disgraced former Los Angeles police officer. Dorner was terminated from the police department for making false allegations against his field training officer. Dorner went on a revenge-fueled rampage against police officers and their significant others from February 3-12, 2013, leading to the largest manhunt in Los Angeles history.

With a personal arsenal of high-powered, high-tech weaponry, Dorner murdered three police officers plus another individual. He wounded three more law enforcement professionals and exchanged gunfire with police on multiple occasions. He also participated in auto theft, kidnapping, and breaking into a mountain cabin. It was in this mountain cabin that authorities found Dorner and a gunfight ensued. Dorner died of a self-inflicted gunshot wound to the head. *(Gofford, 2014)*

If there was a template for a spree killing, Dorner's case would fit perfectly in numerous categories. There were multiple victims in separate locations; the spree was one continuing event; numerous crimes were part of the attempt to elude police; the offender was a fugitive with a huge police presence amassed to capture him; and when his abandoned truck was located, it contained the debris and detritus of his crimes, such as burned guns, spent ammunition, a tent, a knife, and maps.

Other spree killers of note are Gianni Versace's killer, Andrew Cunanan, and Lee Malvo and John Muhammad, the Washington, D.C.-area Beltway Snipers of 2002.

Note 2: In 2008, the FBI, along with other experts, discussed whether the concept of spree murder should be eliminated from the jargon. This was due to the fact they could not agree on adequately addressing the cooling-off period that occurs between killings. They proffered that the bifurcated mass murder concept be substituted. This writer disagrees with eliminating the term spree killer. *(Hickey, 2014, lecture notes)*

Serial Murder

The last category is serial murder. This is the killing of two or more persons over a period of time ranging from weeks to years, with an emotional cooling-off period. This type of murder is usually sexually related, and the offender obtains sexual gratification from the stalking, torture, and/or keeping of trophies from the victims. The killer has an all-invasive, intrusive fantasy life, replete with mind pictures of extremely violent sex, which drives this offender to commit heinous acts of an unspeakable nature. *(Douglas, et al., 1988)*

Although numerous researchers, academics, and criminologists have developed modalities addressing serial murder, the FBI arguably was the first major law enforcement agency to acknowledge the concept of serial murder. The FBI also undertook the first major study of this type of offender, developing a serial murder motivational model as well as establishing a national clearing house and database addressing this phenomenon.

The FBI model determined there are primarily two distinct types of offenders: disorganized and organized. If there are indices of both at a crime scene, it is labeled mixed. *(Douglas, et al., 1988)* These two types of killers are on opposite ends of the homicidal continuum, with nothing in common except the end result: murder. An example of each follows:

Disorganized

The following is a case study gleaned from Crime Scene and Profile Characteristics of Organized and Disorganized Murders. *(Campbell and DeNivi, 2004)*

Richard Chase was a slovenly, emaciated, drug-abusing psychotic who spent a number of stints in mental health facilities. He lived alone in a run-down hovel, and was often seen wandering neighborhoods aimlessly. Chase was so fascinated with blood that during one time period in mental health care, the other patients called him Dracula.

Chase would stalk and kill small animals, drink their blood, and mutilate them, experimenting with the body parts. In one instance, he was found naked and covered in rabbit blood in the desert. He informed police the blood was his and it was draining from his body. He feared he was going to disintegrate. He was subsequently placed in an institution. It was after this hospitalization that the killings began.

Crime 1

Chase began his serial murder rampage with a drive-by shooting in Sacramento, California, on December 29, 1977. Approximately two weeks later, he attempted to enter a home, but left after finding the door locked. He later told authorities that a locked door meant he was unwelcome, but an unlocked door was an invitation to enter.

Murder 2

One evening, at approximately 6:00 p.m., a husband returned from work and found his wife's body in a closet. She had been dead since morning. She had been shot in the head four times, then disemboweled with a butcher knife found in the home. There were slash wounds to the breasts and the internal organs were mutilated. Garbage was strewn about the house, the victim had animal feces in her mouth, and there was evidence that her blood had been consumed by the offender.

Crime 3

A house burglary occurred the same day in the same neighborhood as the second killing. Garbage was thrown about the home, and there were indications that the perpetrator had urinated and defecated on female clothing.

Crime 4

The carcass of a dog was found two days later in the same neighborhood. The animal had been shot, and it was later learned the bullet was from the same gun as the first series of murders. The dog had been disemboweled.

Murder 3

A female waiting for a ride noticed a man's car in her neighbor's driveway four days after the second killing. She noticed the car was gone moments later. Feeling concerned, she went to the neighbor's home and found the bodies of a male friend, her female neighbor, and the neighbor's child. A twenty-two-month-old infant was missing.

A bullet was found in the crib, along with what appeared to be skull fragments and brain matter. As similar material was found in the tub, officers surmised that the infant's body had been washed prior to being taken from the scene. The female victim had been slashed and mutilated, disemboweled from breast to pelvis. Internal organs had been removed and examined, and a foreign object had been inserted into a body cavity, causing massive damage.

A profile developed by the FBI suggested the offender would be a Caucasian male, thin, and undernourished. He would reside alone in a slovenly, ill-kept abode, and evidence of his crimes would be present among the debris. The suspect would have a history of drug use and mental illness. He would be an unemployed or under-employed loner who lived in the area and could easily walk to the crime scenes.

With this profile, police narrowed their search and focused on a twenty-seven-year-old man named Richard Chase. He was in possession of a gun that matched the murder weapon. Also found in his apartment were body parts, including those of the missing infant, with evidence of cannibalism and blood-drinking.

Chase was found guilty of six counts of first degree murder and sentenced to death in California. He died in prison of a self-induced drug overdose. *(Campbell and DeNevi, 2004)*

Profile Characteristics of Organized and Disorganized Murderers
(Campbell and DeNevi, 2004)

Characteristic	Organized (e.g. Bundy)	Disorganized (e.g. Chase)
Intelligence	Above average	Below average
Social interactions	Competent	Inadequate
Sexual interactions	Competent, numerous experiences	Inadequate, isolated
Employment	Employability skills	Unskilled, often unemployed
Living arrangements	Often lives with partner, dates frequently	Lives alone or with inattentive parent
Automobile	Nice car	Often walks or has older, unattractive vehicle
Appearance	Good hygiene, well-dressed	Slovenly, unkempt

Organized

The following is a case study gleaned from Crime Scene and Profile Characteristics of Organized and Disorganized Murderers (Campbell and DeNevi), and Ted Bundy Multiagency Investigative Team Report (FBI).

Theodore (Ted) Bundy is the polar opposite of Richard Chase and possibly the epitome of an apex predator. Like the orca, bald eagle, or Kodiak bear – all apex predators in their respective milieus – Bundy, and others of his ilk, is a killer so skilled at murder that he fits into a select category of organized killers. Bundy was a suave, verbal, erudite crisis center phone volunteer. He was a well-coiffed, handsome law student, outgoing, and often seen in the company of members of the upper class. He claimed numerous girlfriends and was an extremely popular individual.

According to multiple sources, Bundy's offenses were generally very well-planned, often far in advance of the actual crime. He would follow a pattern of feigning an injury, often complete with a fake cast on his arm and asking for assistance, or he would act like a law enforcement officer. After persuading his victim to come with him, he would get her into his crime-equipped Volkswagen that featured no passenger seat and doors that could not be unlocked from inside. He would then strike her with a crowbar and handcuff her in the passenger seat area. He often drove for hours with the victim in the car, finally arriving at a predetermined dump site, where he would strangle her with a ligature while raping her.

Bundy's behaviors and actions fit the profile of an extremely organized killer. He made many return visits to numerous crime scenes. He would discard much of the victim's property, taking care to keep some "souvenirs" such as jewelry, rings, and bracelets, often giving them to other women as gifts. He maintained multiple body disposal sites and followed the investigation in the media.

Lastly, he maintained a "murder kit" consisting of props and tools needed to successfully complete a homicide. The kit consisted of a mask, duct tape, ice picks, ligatures and gloves, as well as other items. Bundy also modified his vehicle to better conceal and contain his victims. A well-developed ruse aided him in approaching victims in a non-threatening manner.

This prolific killer claimed thirty female victims. Bundy was put to death in Florida for the killing of two coeds and the slaying of a twelve-year-old girl he abducted on her way home from school. These crimes were committed when he was a fugitive, and the stress caused him to "go off script." Risking apprehension, Bundy entered a sorority house on the campus of Florida State University, where he bludgeoned two coeds to death while they slept. Out of control, he also bit the two victims. As other coeds returned to the house, he bludgeoned three others to near death. Days later, he abducted an adolescent girl, raped, and murdered her. Her remains were found three months later. *(Campbell and DeNevi, 2004) (U.S. Department of Justice/FBI, 1992)*

Crime Scene Differences between Organized and Disorganized Murderers
(Campbell and DeNevi, 2004)

Feature	Organized (e.g. Bundy)	Disorganized (e.g. Chase)
Offense	Well-planned	Spontaneous, blitz attack
Victim	Targeted stranger	Known to offender
Locale	Targeted, unrelated to perpetrator	Known to offender
Crime scene	Controlled	Sloppy, chaotic
Restraints	Planned, part of the crime	Usually not used
Weapons	Possesses a "murder kit"	Weapon of opportunity
Body	Transported, hidden	Left at scene in sight
Taken from scene	"Souvenirs" such as jewelry	"Trophy" such as a body part
Media	Follows media report of crime closely; might return to scene	Does not follow media report of crime; rarely returns to scene
Law enforcement	Police "groupie"; inserts self into investigation	Avoids police

Serial Killing for Profit

Dirk Gibson, in his book *Serial Killing for Profit*, offers that the commercial aspect of serial killing has been overlooked for too long. Gibson writes, "Profit-motivated serial slayings ought to be included in our definitions and understanding of serial murder." He goes on to suggest that "commercial serial murder is often excluded from consideration due to motive." (Non-sexual)

Gibson addresses twelve case studies ranging in differences from Ray and Faye Copeland, who murdered transient farm workers for social security checks, to H. H. Holmes (aka Herman Mudgett), who preyed upon unaccompanied young women for their paychecks and property rights. Gibson includes Richard Ramirez, the infamous Night Stalker, who killed, in part, in the act of burglary to offset a $1,500 weekly cocaine habit, as well as Raymond Fernandez and Martha Beck, who murdered lonely women for money and possessions. (Gibson, 2010)

Gibson shows convincingly that there is a specific killer type who is primarily motivated by money. And while his lobbying to expand the definition of serial killing by adding another grouping to the two existing categories is admirable, appreciated, and necessary, his suggestion still falls short of this writer's theory: that there is yet another type of multiple killer on the homicidal landscape who does not neatly fit into any previously established categories.

Is There Another Type of Killer Out There?

Lt. Jon Priest, a member of the Denver Police Department's homicide bureau, offered a seminar during the 2010 National Homicide Investigators Association Conference in Green Bay, Wisconsin, on the murder of popular Denver Broncos football player Darrent Williams and related killings. Williams was murdered in a drive-by shooting after an altercation at a nightclub following a game.

Lt. Priest discussed the case and the involvement of the Tre Tre Crips street gang. One of the main actors in this gang was a man named Brian Hicks, and it was learned Hicks was involved in at least nine killings uncovered in the course of the Williams investigation.

During the presentation, Lt. Priest was asked why Hicks is not considered a serial killer. The lieutenant answered that although Hicks had killed many individuals, he was more of what Priest would consider to be a pattern killer: murdering many in a sequence, but with no overt similarities with the serial murder typology. It was this discussion that led this author to believe yet another diverse category of multiple murder was needed in the lexicon of criminology.

Profile of a New Killer Type

This new profile of murderer will have the following attributes that differentiate him from other established typologies: This type of offender is an individual (or a team) who engages in a series of murders over an indeterminate period of time for the specific purpose of furthering a criminal enterprise, i.e. gang/drug cartel, organized crime family, to obtain personal illicit gain, or as the preferred outcome of a professional killer.

The killer often acts at the behest of another, and there is no true cooling-off period between each killing except when dictated by those who order the killings or as the need arises. This killer most likely exhibits sociopathic traits such as callous disregard and/or no concern for the victim or pain inflicted. Non-traditional weapons are often used such as machine guns, bombs, and grenades, along with regular weaponry to include handguns, shotguns, and knives.

As many serial murders are sexual in nature and have a tactile component, these killings can often be considered "non-touching," employing pistols and bombs, as well as drive-by shootings. There appears to be a simple need for expedience rather than the existence of fantasy in these killings. This is not to say this type of killer does not enjoy the act. The killings can range from a single act to multicide. Finally, there is a code-like concept within the structure of the deviant organization. The code is to never cooperate with authorities or risk death.

Although there might be torture and mutilation to/ or removal of sexual organs, the murders are very rarely sexual in nature. Rather, the killings are either to collect debts, silence an informant/witness, avenge a perceived threat, or send a message to a rival and/or rid the organization of nonproductive members. *(Drake, et al., 2011)*

Sadism and Murder Are Not Always Sexual

Despite the fact that many of these types of murders have the markings of sadism and there certainly could be a sexual component, there are other categories of sadism that are more conducive to this type of murder and often confused for sexual sadism. *(Hazelwood, 2001)*

According to former FBI Special Agent Roy Hazelwood, there are seven types of sadistic behaviors, five of which could easily be utilized and are self-explanatory:

1) Non-sexual sadism (sadism that does not sexually arouse the perpetrator)

2) Cruelty during a crime

3) Pathological group behavior. This is when three or more individuals engage in a single crime. Usually the killing, abuse, and torture is done by each offender to impress the others with ferocity and "badness."

4) Revenge-motivated cruelty. This is often engaged in by members of organized crime groups. The Mafia has a history of extreme cruelty toward informants, as do Mexican cartels and other criminal enterprises.

5) Post-mortem mutilation

This yet-unnamed typology consists of some of the attributes of many multiple killings: there are myriad areas that branch off into a different mindset, behavioral system, and basis for killing. It also appears this type of offender would exhibit sociopathic-like tendencies, as well as be clearly cognizant of right and wrong, but acts without conscience and cares little for the consequences. These offenders can be charming and glib, but also malevolent and extremely dangerous. To a person, these killers are ruthless, remorseless, and engage in killing with callous concern. Many of these offenders will have prior criminal records and are deeply entrenched in the criminal lifestyle. They are habitués of the dark underworld of violence.

Race or ethnicity are of no import in this category of crime, as the killers can be members of a black street gang, a white-dominated outlaw motorcycle club, a Hispanic drug cartel, or an ethnic organized crime group such as Russian, Jamaican, Vietnamese, Italian, or any other established group. They could be members of an extremely organized prison gang, such as the Aryan Brotherhood, Mexican Mafia, and Nuestra Familia. They can also be a rogue assassin bent on obtaining as much ill-gotten gain as possible. *(Klienknecht, 1999)*

A factor to be considered in these killings is the concept of the gang mentality. The Hamilton Police Service (Canada) breaks the concept into multiple components:

Being respected – Being respected is essentially being feared, and is based upon one's reputation for being volatile and dangerous. This includes the idea of "do or die" for the group. There is a deep disrespect for rivals. One way to gain respect is disdain, disrespect, and lack of fear of rivals. No insult goes unanswered. No act of disrespect is ignored.

Problems are handled from within – With a stable of members willing to engage in murder, there is no need to go outside of the organization to settle disputes.

Disregard for the rights of others – Showing any empathy can be ruinous to an individual's reputation. *(Hamilton Police Service Fact Sheet, 2014)*

Abnormal Homicide and Gang Involvement

Abnormal homicides are those that fall into the category of multiple murder, sexual murder, or serial killings. The authors of a recent study found that few gang members engage in sexual or serial murder. However, mass murder is one of the abnormal homicides that gang members are potentially more likely to perpetrate, often as a result of drive-by shootings. Gang involvement is relatively low even in cases that are prone to produce mass fatalities at a single location, time and place. Nearly 25 percent of victims in drive-by shootings are innocent victims. *(Delisi, et al., 2013)*

The Prison Gang Aspect

Author Tony Rafael, in his in-depth study of the Mexican Mafia (EME), looks at this type of killer more from a universal, illicit-type of business operative. These individuals have given their all to a "family and a love of violence, along with a renegade love to kill."

Rafael categorizes Mexican Mafia killings (and this can be attributed to other ethnic gangs) as falling into six categories, many which fit the new pattern type profile alluded to in this article. They are:

Unproductive members – When an EME member stops his productivity in terms of making money or meeting his gang commitments, the gang is "cleaning up the books," and getting rid of "dead wood."

Uncooperative drug dealers – If a street dealer refuses to pay his "street tax," he is given the opportunity to relinquish his assets (drugs, cars, money, etc.). If he declines, he is murdered.

Informants – Members of EME are forbidden to snitch or talk with authorities. If the investigators develop paperwork about the interview, the informant is killed.

Ethnic cleansing – EME members will, at all cost, attempt to keep African Americans from their neighborhoods. Intimidation is the first tool utilized. If it fails, murder is the sanction.

Other prisoners – Given that the Mexican Mafia is a prison-based organized crime group, many of their assassinations take place within institutions. These killings are difficult to carry out because if a killing occurs, there is a lockdown and gang business suffers. However, if a rival inmate or a recalcitrant gang member needs to be killed, the gang will select a member who is dispensable. That individual will do the killing.

Personals – These killings are undertaken because members feel they have been disrespected in some way. An example is if someone is dating the EME member's wife. The wife is too valuable to murder, so the man is killed.

Case Studies

1. Although not a bona fide member of any highly organized group, the late Richard (the Iceman) Kuklinski was a rogue killer for numerous Mafia families and is considered organized crime's most prolific "hit man." Kuklinski killed with no apparent loyalty to anyone but himself. *(Carlo, 2006)* His services were for sale to the highest bidder.

Authorities opine that this man alone killed hundreds of individuals in any way imaginable, from crossbows to poison, to feeding his victims to rats. His killing career was mainly for the purpose of maintaining order within various Mafia families. Kuklinski tortured many victims, filming their demise for proof of his killings as well as to hone his skills for future lethal endeavors. There is some indication he watched video tapes of some of the killings "in order to feel something," as well as to critique his own killing techniques.

Another case study can assist readers in visualizing the brutality, focus, and machine-like killing ability of this type of offender. Consider the following:

2. Recent history indicates that drug border war violence between Mexican cartels has spilled into the United States, reaching an apex in the city of Laredo, Texas. According to authorities, three American teenagers were recruited by the Zetas, the enforcement wing of one of Mexico's largest drug organizations, and used to kill those deemed expendable. The teens were furnished a house, autos, modern military weapons, and money. They would wait, party, play video games, and generally act like most American teenagers. But, when the Zetas called, the boys needed to follow orders and murder the assigned target. According to police, the trio of teen assassins have killed many people in various ways, each murder more brutal than the previous. *(Esquire, 2009)*

One of the teens, who is currently incarcerated, spoke with nonchalance about his role in the numerous killings during a television interview. He expressed no sorrow, grief, or remorse. As far as he was concerned, murder was simply business as usual, and prison is simply a hazard of the job.

Although most large metropolitan areas, urban counties, and densely populated states can be breeding grounds for this type of killer, three cases offer a template for further study.

3. An example of this type of killer is the case of Chicago-based Vice Lords member Terrence Richardson. Richardson rose to the rank of 5 Star Elite within his gang. For a time, he was the ranking non-incarcerated Vice Lord. During the course of his gang career, Richardson was placed on Chicago's Most Wanted List for what one investigator suggested were twelve unsolved homicides, including the drive-by shooting of a fourteen-year-old girl walking home from school.

Richardson traveled to Green Bay, Wisconsin, in an effort to expand his lucrative drug trafficking business. While attempting to collect a drug debt, this killer sexually assaulted the girlfriend of an associate and then attempted to shoot the associate to death. Richardson was apprehended before he could flee back to Illinois. He is now serving an eighty-year sentence as a result of his most recent crime spree.

In a situation of true irony, a number of Richardson's family members were murdered as retaliation for Terrence giving police a plethora of information on the Vice Lords in an effort to lessen his sentence. None of these murdered family members, including his mother, were involved in the gang. *(Author's professional records)*

4. The second case also occurred in Chicago. In late 2010 and early 2011, three Hispanic men allegedly robbed and murdered at least twelve drug dealers. Arturo Ibarra (shot by police during one of his post-murder chases), Augustin Toscano, and Raul Segura were charged in a series of multiple murders over a number of months. According to police, these three individuals engaged in

a multiplicity of killings in order to reap the benefits of underworld actions. They engaged in virtually all types of multiple murder, including mass (quadruple) murder, two triple murders, and finally a double killing. All were perpetrated in an effort to make "easy money" by stealing other drug dealers' profits." *(Chicago Tribune, 2011)*

5. A case from south Florida speaks to yet another example. During the height of the cocaine wars in Miami in the 1990s, drug "queen pin" Griselda Blanco was suspected of ordering in excess of 200 murders. Her personal hit squad, called Los Pistoleros, was expected to carry out these killings in brutal fashion. The group would target a victim, kill the person in outrageous fashion, cut the corpse open, fold it into a box, and mail it to the family. *(Maxim, 2013)*

This type of killer is definitely different than offenders covered in the original six typologies. The killers in this category are varied in mindset, motive, and method of operation, but seem to kill out of an all-consuming greed or loyalty to a larger entity. The terminology is not sufficient to describe the Kuklinskis and Richardsons of the world. What is an adequate name for this type of multiple murderer? Is it pattern killer, as Lt. Priest suggests? A multiple-victim assassin? A series killer? A non-sexual repeat killer? An episodic killer? Or finally, a serial executioner? Or, should this crime simply be added to what could be a trilogy of serial murder: 1) Classical/Sexual; 2) Spree; 3) Non-sexual/Entrepreneurial?

6. A final example is the case of Van Brett Watkins. In 1999, Rae Carruth, then a member of the NFL's Carolina Panthers, hired Watkins to kill his girlfriend, Cherica Adams, after failing to convince her to have an abortion.

For $6,000, Watkins (aka New York), a street-savvy thug, pulled up next to Adams's car and opened fire. A barrage of bullets killed her, but not before she was able to tell a 911 operator that Carruth pulled his car in front of hers, while a second car stopped next to her and fired. Doctors were able to Adams's baby, but he is severely handicapped after being without oxygen for over an hour while his mother died.

In an interview with the *Charlotte Observer* as well as the television show *The Killer Speaks*, Watkins stated he murdered at least four other people for money: two in New York, one in Miami, and one in Atlanta. He went on to offer he was hired by women who were either in abusive relationships or simply tired of the men they wanted killed.

Watkins, a boastful killer, said in discussing his beating of another man nearly to death, "You can feel the high of it. Like shooting a gun or driving 100 miles per hour."

Carruth was released from prison in October of 2018. Watkins won't be released until at least 2046.

Conclusion

Enzo Yaksic, the founder of the Serial Homicide Expertise and Information Sharing Collaborative offers:

"To this day, the majority of criminologists protest including gang killings and professional murders in serial homicide offender databases because these offenses typically occur alongside functional or instrumental violence. If killing is a means of conflict resolution, endorsed by others, motivated strictly by financial gain, the byproduct of provocation or is committed out of convenience, revenge or survival, the offender is often deliberately excluded from serial offender research samples.

"Because these offenders have understandable, conventional, and logical motivations, they are erroneously viewed as being different than killers yearning to repetitively relish in causing death. To most researchers, killing serially implies that murder must be the primary objective on a killer's quest toward psychological gratification and not used as a response to situational factors. A significant aspect of the offender's life is dedicated to the process of serial killing with an emphasis placed on fantasy, planning, victim pursuit, and rumination, aspects that gang members and contract killers do not overtly engage.

"The antiquated mindset of some researchers is that an offender must display a sexual component at the crime scene to qualify for a serial killer classification. The terms 'sexual murder' and 'serial murder' have become indistinguishable over the years while researchers fail to acknowledge that the serial sexual killer is but one of the many subsets of multiple murderer.

"As demonstrated, criminologists are overly restrictive in their narrow interpretations of what constitutes a serial killer. As such, we have overlooked the evolving nature of serial homicide and ignored how serial killers are molded by social conditions, cultural changes and external pressures. Establishing another class of multiple murder is essential to the advancement of the science of serial homicide, and would have the full support of the Serial Homicide Expertise and Information Sharing Collaborative."

Murder typologies are an important and necessary tool to many in the criminal justice field. They assist in gathering statistics and in developing profiles, as well as numerous other uses for investigators, prison staff, parole personnel, and researchers. In order for these tools to be efficient, they need to be consistent. A disservice is being done by not developing another class of multiple murder to add to the aforementioned six typologies. Criminology must expand, grow and modernize, or be damned to a dusty science.

Sources of Information

Author's Personal/Professional Notes on Terrance Richardson.

Author's Personal/Professional Notes on Organized and Disorganized Offenders.

Brown, Ethan, (2008), *Searching for the Godmother, Maxim Magazine,* New York, Dennis Publishing.

Campbell, John, DeNevi, Don, (2004), *Profilers (1st Edition),* New York, Prometheus Press.

Carlo, Phil, (2006) *Ice Man: Confessions of a Mafia Killer (1st Edition)* New York, St. Martin's Press.

Delisi, Matt, Spruill, James O. Vaughn, Michael, Trulson, Chad. (2013) *Do Gang Members Commit Abnormal Homicides? (1st Edition) American Journal of Criminal Justice,* Springer.

Dittrich, Luke, (2009) *4 Days on the Border, Esquire Magazine,* New York, Hearst Magazine Division.

Drake, Dallas, Snater, Casey, Brooks, Kelsey, Butts, Casi (2011) *Investigating Mexican Cartel-Style Homicides in the United States,* Minneapolis, Center for Homicide Research.

Douglas, John, Burgess, Anne, Burgess, Allen, Ressler, Robert. (2013) *Crime Classification Manual: A Standard System for Investigating and Classifying Violent Crime (3rd Edition)* Hoboken, N.J., John Wiley and Sons.

Duwe, Grant, (2007) *A History: Mass Murder in the United States, (1st Edition),* Jefferson, North Carolina, McFarland.

Franklin, Tony, (2011) *Mexican Mafia, (1st Edition)* New York, Encounter Press, Personal Correspondence with Author.

Gibson, Dirk, (2010) *Serial Killing for Profit: Multiple Murder for Money, (1st Edition)* Santa Barbara, California, Praeger.

Gofford, Christopher, (2014), *Los Angeles Times, The Manhunt for Christopher Dorner.*

Gorner, Jeremy, Meisner, James, (2011) *Chicago Tribune, Hardworking Roofer or Brutal Killer.* Chicago, Tribune Publishing.

Hamilton (Canada) Police Services Fact Sheet (2014) No Author Attributed.

Hazelwood, Roy, Michaud, Stephen (2001) *Dark Dreams: Sexual Violence, Homicide and the Criminal Mind (1st Edition)* New York, St. Martin's Press.

Hickey, Eric, Lecture Notes, *Behavioral Characteristics of Multiple Homicide Offenders Training,* American Institute for the Advancement of Forensic Studies, (June 5, 2014), St. Paul, Minnesota.

Keppel, Robert, (1997) *Signature Killers, (1st Edition),* New York Pocket Books.

Klienknecht, William, (1996) *The New Ethnic Mobs, (1st Edition),* New York, The Free Press.

Ted Bundy Multiagency Investigative Team Report, (1992) United States Department of Justice, Government Printing Office.

Ressler, Robert, Burgess, Ann, Douglas, *(1988) Sexual Homicide: Patterns and Motives, (1st Edition),* New York, Lexington Books.

Acknowledgements

As with all of my works, a tip of the hat to my father, the late Detective Captain Norman Daniels, Green Bay Police Department, for showing me there are many victims to murder.

To my "murder buddies": Dallas Drake, Center for Homicide Research; Mike Arntfield, University of Western Ontario; Enzo Yaksic, Serial Murder Information Sharing Collaborative; and Steve Giannangelo, Special Agent (ret.).

Connie Fellman, freelance writer, for early input and editing.

The staff at the Brown County Library's Ashwaubenon Branch, for their daily patience, computer assistance and overall help.

Sandy Hahn, longtime friend and editor.

Chris Heil, for overall support.

Joe Nelson, news reporter, for his information on the Bradshaw murders.

Rick Luell, Special Agent, Wisconsin Department of Justice (ret.), for his assistance on the Leesa Jo Shaner case and his impetus in writing this book.

Chris Zunker, Sauk County Sheriff's Office, and the entire agency for their assistance on the Mary Johnson case.

Sasha Reid and her nerdy serial murder hobby.

Mike Dauplaise and Bonnie Groessl at M&B Global Solutions Inc., publishers and editors, for again making my goal a reality.

Of course, my family. Just for being there.

About the Author

Steve Daniels retired after twenty-six years in the criminal justice system, the last twelve as a high-risk parole agent working with extremely violent and dangerous offenders. During that career, Steve and a colleague interviewed and researched nearly two hundred murderers in an effort to develop a working profile for criminal justice professionals.

After beginning his correctional career as a social worker at the Drug Abuse Correctional Center, Steve transferred into the probation and parole field as an agent with a general caseload. He developed the Habitual Offender Supervision Team in 1992 along with another agent, focusing on a high-risk, intensive caseload for assaultive, dangerous, and violent offenders.

Steve Daniels

Steve worked on some of the most notorious cased in northeast Wisconsin history, including pre-sentence investigations on individuals involved in the Tom Monfils murder case at the James River paper mill in Green Bay,

Wisconsin; a woman charged with murdering two elderly women in Kewaunee County, Wisconsin; the killing of two police officers; and an attempted murder committed by a man suspected of twelve kills in Chicago. Steve also supervised armed robbers, sex offenders, and offenders with roots deep in the criminal lifestyle.

Steve is a charter member and has served multiple terms on the board of directors of the Cold Case Review Team for the Wisconsin Association of Homicide Investigators, assisting agencies with old, unsolved homicides. The association presented Steve with its Public Service Award in 1989, the President's Award in 2003 and 2006, and the Distinguished Career Award in 2006. Steve was instrumental in the development of the association's Cold Case Review Team and is a nationally known trainer in the areas of Compound Dwellers: Dangerous Groups Living Off the Grid; Analyzing Pre-Killing Behavior; and Understanding the Typologies of Murder. He has been a faculty member at the National Academy of Corrections in Boulder, Colorado, for the course "Managing Gangs and Disruptive Groups," and has offered training for the FBI in its regional conferences on terrorism.

Steve is the author of the book *Harry: A Study of Teenage Mass Murderers*, numerous articles on various types of homicide, and is the coordinator of a nationally recognized annual homicide conference. He will be a featured expert on an upcoming multi-disc DVD series on serial murder.

Steve resides in Green Bay, Wisconsin, with his wife, Nancy. He has two sons, Chris and Joe, and four grandchildren, Joshua, Isaac, Zooey and Penelope.

Made in the USA
Middletown, DE
26 March 2019